LESSONS IN STYLE

MESSI

PRAISE FOR MESSI: LESSONS IN STYLE

"Reading this playful portrait of Leo Messi reminded me how extraordinary every minute was that I spent by his side, seeing him training and playing for four years. Perhaps the best way to recall this privilege is with some words I recently came across by the poet Maya Angelou: 'I've learnt that people will forget what you said, people will forget what you did, but people will never forget how you made them feel.'"

PEP GUARDIOLA

"Jordi Puntí is a beautiful writer and a Barcelona fan who has watched Messi's entire career and is in love with him. There's nobody better to write this book – which doesn't aim to explain Messi (impossible anyway) but to enjoy him. It's a lovely, joyous read."

SIMON KUPER, co-author of *Soccernomics*

"This portrait of Messi, forged in a thoughtful, virtuoso style, captures not only his greatness, but also allows us to use the life of an icon to rethink the state of contemporary writing."

OSCAR BROX, *Revista Détour*

"Jordi Puntí's stunning tribute to Lionel Messi will captivate football aficionados as well as fans of fine writing... He roams around his subject, like Messi himself in the free attacking role he played in the glory years when Pep Guardiola was managing Barcelona."

IAN SANSOM, *Spectator*

LESSONS IN STYLE

MESSI

JORDI PUNTÍ

Translated from the Catalan by Peter Bush

First published in **Catalan** in 2018 by Grup Editorial 62, s.l.u.,
Editorial Empúries, Peu de la Creu, 4, 08001 Barcelona

Published in **English** in 2018 by **Short Books**,
Unit 316, ScreenWorks, 22 Highbury Grove,
London, N5 2ER

This paperback edition published in 2019 by **Short Books**

10 9 8 7 6 5 4 3 2 1

Cover design by Two Associates
Cover image copyright © David Ramos/Getty Images

ISBN: 978-1-78072-415-7

A CIP catalogue record for this book
is available from the British Library.

Printed and bound in Great Britain
by Clays Ltd, Elcograf S.p.A.

Also by Jordi Puntí

Original Catalan Fiction

Pell d'armadillo

Animals tristos

Maletes perdudes

Els Castellans

Això no és Amèrica

Original Fiction Translated into English

Lost Luggage

This is Not America

CONTENTS

"How great it would be to be him for five seconds, just to know what it feels like."

Javier Mascherano

"I sometimes wonder whether Messi is human."

Thierry Henry

"Messi is the best player in the world. An injured Messi is the next best player in the world."

Jorge Valdano

"Sir Isaac Newton from above looks down and says: 'About that gravity thing, I was wrong, Messi is right. He teases gravity.'"

Ray Hudson

"Barça is always dependent on Messi's happiness."

Ramon Besa

FOREWORD

THERE ARE MANY WAYS TO DECIDE who your favourite player is. The picture-card you've kept from when you were a kid, hidden in a box like an exiled king and that you revisit only very occasionally when gripped by an attack of nostalgia. That faded shirt with his name on the back, the one you've worn a thousand times and that, for some mysterious reason, always brings you good luck in cup finals. YouTube videos of his moves and goals, that some madman like you – but with more time on his hands – has put together so you can see them in a permanent loop. There was a time when Romário was my favourite player, and I kept a video tape of the 30 goals he promised (and scored) in his first season. More than once, if Barça were losing or on a bad run, I'd watch that video as you might take a painkiller. And it worked. I'm referring to the '93-'94 season, when Romário won the *Pichichi* Trophy, was top scorer in La Liga. Nowadays we'd think that's a quite normal number, because Leo Messi has spoiled us, but at the time it seemed like a supernatural phenomenon. Many of those goals looked as if they'd been *invented* – as if nobody could have done that before: in his first *El Clásico* in Barcelona, he scored a hat-trick and produced his *cola de vaca*, "cow's tail" trick, where he stopped the ball dead, then dragged it round and past Rafael Alkorta; his chips and six-yard sprints; his gentle, but precise touches or swivelling runs; or the way he lurks in the background tracking the ball, like a predator about to pounce... This may sound blasphemous but when I review that repertoire, it feels as if I'm watching a trailer for what we've subsequently witnessed over the last ten years. As if Johan Cruyff's Dream Team had been the curtain-raiser for the main show starring Xavi, Iniesta, Puyol, Busquets, Messi and company, especially in the years they were coached by Pep Guardiola and Tito Vilanova.

Although the calendar predisposes us to see football as a linear phenomenon, developing over time and renewed every game, with the intrigue of hearing the results or seeing the champions who must start from zero at the beginning of a new season, I like to think of it as a territory where past and present interweave, and sometimes – as in T.S. Eliot's famous lines – even hold sway over the future. Precise examples of these manias of mine will surface throughout the following pages. Football is also the territory of memory and we find it exciting because it allows us to travel back in time, revisit great players, forget lost finals, stand in our heroes' shoes and mix memory and desire. There are real goals that truly never went in, that hit the post or missed by inches, and only years later, another player in another game completed them in my memory. He scored a goal, but in truth he was scoring two: one in the present, that he celebrated, and another in the past that only I celebrated. What I mean is that football is even more entertaining when seen as a parallel world. A religion, if you like, or a philosophical system, or a struggle against chance. Everyone sees a different game, we are all coaches, and basically a professional chess player and a poet never see the same game.

But let's go back to the beginning.

In my case, among the many reasons why I decided that Leo Messi is my favourite player of all time is the fact that I sometimes dream about him. As far as I can remember, I had only dreamt previously about the occasional move by Ronaldinho, or some composite game, when I couldn't make out the players, on the eve of a Barcelona–Real Madrid match (which we were winning, naturally). On the other hand, I have dreamt about Messi several times. I have dreamt about him as if I was his father and was serving him breakfast at the bar in some cafeteria, no doubt in Rosario (where I've never been). I have dreamt about him as if we were linked by blood, as if I were a big brother sitting with him in an empty bus parked outside a deserted football field. I have dreamt he was scoring amazing goals, dribbling in gravity-defying runs that unfolded before me like a wondrous aurora borealis. Messi was often alone in these dreams, and I imagine a Freudian psychiatrist could use these elements to tell me more about myself than about the Argentine, but I interpret it – I *want* to interpret it – as a connection beyond the present, a relationship that takes place in the ethereal world of the unconscious. He doesn't know this, but the way he plays has often made me happy, in both the reality of the present and the fictional world of dreams.

This book came into being some time ago as my

individual attempt to extend this happiness, rather than to try and explain it. Italo Calvino defined the potential features of literature in the 21st century and it turns out that, in his way, Messi has them all: lightness, quickness, exactitude, visibility and multiplicity (I'll say more about this later).

The football picture-cards I collected in my childhood featured two images: one of the footballer quietly posing for the photo on the turf, and the other of him in action, shooting or controlling a ball – or saving it if he was a goalkeeper. Messi exemplifies better than anyone else both these states: hovering quietly in the middle of the pitch, moving slowly, then suddenly launching into a controlled burst of speed. Perhaps these pages could be defined as a picture-card in motion, one of those short internet videos that define a whole move in ten seconds. I'll simply enact the movements with my words: vaguely inspired by Raymond Queneau's model, I will try to sketch some *exercises* – or *lessons* – *in style* suggested by the figure of Leo Messi. Deconstructing Messi. Rewriting Messi. He will be the protagonist of each text, the thousand faces of style, and my task will consist of capturing in these pages the beauty, the hunger, the genius, the modernity, the obsession and the instinct, among many other things, of a footballer who is the best in history. It's very likely, then, that *Messi*, *goal* and *Barça* will be the words that crop up most often – and, sure, *Argentina*, as well – but that's hardly surprising now, is it?

These pages are blessed by a happy condition: they are unfinished. They are a work in progress, a game that is still being played. While Messi continues as a professional footballer, some sentences can change – will have to change. I don't just mean the statistics that coldly sum up his unique record, but the emotion, the enthusiasm, the ability to innovate in every game and find solutions with the ball that hitherto had never even been contemplated in the world of football. Like an artist capable of inventing a colour because the ones he has don't suffice.

I'm rewriting this foreword exactly one year after the first edition was published in Catalan in April 2018. In those twelve months Messi has experienced the disappointment of not winning the World Cup in Russia with his national team – the top target for an Argentinian – but with FC Barcelona he has left us a series of memorable performances that once more prompt fans and journalists to wonder: what is there he can't do?

To give an example, I'll mention the victory against Tottenham Hotspur, in the Champions League group stage, October 2018. Barça notched up yet another win at Wembley (2-4) with a stellar performance by Messi that included two goals, two shots against the post and, above all, the feeling that he was leading a team set on playing brilliant and effective football. That night many Brits, who have traditionally viewed the Barça number 10 in a rather insular, patronising manner – as if to say, "what is all the fuss about?" – saw Messi in a new light.

We might think he reserves such excellence for the big occasions but he has also displayed several acts of genius in La Liga that have been celebrated around the world. If I were to choose a moment from this season that will endure in football's collective memory, it would be the game against Betis in the Benito Villamarín stadium (1-4) in March 2019. Messi scored a hat-trick, three goals crowned by a move you want to see time and again: he receives a pass from Rakitic on the edge of the penalty area, slightly to the left, and, as it arrives, he strokes the ball with a fantastic, incredible touch, with nanotechnological precision, sending it rising gently, passing over keeper Pau López, just beyond his reach, and in under the bar. He executes it so simply it's almost as if he hasn't done anything out of this world, but immediately everybody watching knows it is extraordinary, the work of a virtuoso. Despite the painful defeat, even the Betis fans applaud and shout his name: Messi, Messi, Messi! – thanking him for the privilege of seeing him play in the flesh. (By the way, in this same game, Luis Suárez scored a goal after slaloming through the centre, dribbling past four opponents, that had the hallmark of Messi himself. As well as underlining the combination play enjoyed by the two players, it could be seen as something of a surrogate goal: the boldness and inspiration Messi's colleagues feel when they are playing next to him.)

One of the questions that we fans of Barça and football often ask is what Messi will do when he retires. As this sport lives in a present that is renewed with every game, that date right now seems remote and unimaginable, but at the same time we know it's a law of life, and that one day or another that void will hit us. Messi will be 32 as of June 2019, and has been playing in the top flight for over 15 years. I sometimes re-play videos from other periods and I'm suddenly shocked: I see him celebrating goals by the side of Ronaldinho, Villa, Xavi, Iniesta, Alves and Neymar, and I think those images have an unreal aura. Obviously Messi changes, evolves physically and adapts to the new circumstances, but his gestures and style transform him into a kind of Dorian Gray. As if scoring goals and breaking records keeps him young. Indeed one of the outstanding features of this season is the way he is enjoying games, his more gleeful determination and even more competitive spirit, as if he's been liberated from the pressures of age and understands he must relish each moment.

All in all, when I think of the future and try to imagine Messi's final phase, I can't imagine his football going into decline. Over the years he has shown his ability to adapt and discipline himself, as well as an instinctive sense of how to make the most of his talents at any given moment, whether it's swiftness, footballing vision or the analysis of an opponent's weaknesses. Witnessing this constant re-invention, game after game, will also be a great motivation to continue watching him play until the end. And then we will always have our memories and the pleasure of recounting them all over again.

Barcelona, April 2019

1

HIS DEBUT

LET'S FACE IT: LEO MESSI'S DEBUT in Barça's first team was an inconspicuous defeat: 2-0 in a friendly game against FC Porto, to celebrate the inauguration of the Portuguese club's new stadium, the Estádio do Dragão. It was 16 November 2003, a Sunday, and nowadays many Portuguese fans wish Messi had scored the first goal in the history of that pitch, but he didn't. His debut followed the normal pattern that governs the lives of every young footballer. One day they pick you for a first-team friendly, you travel with the seniors, you look at them with a mixture of shyness and admiration, and then the coach gives you twenty minutes at the end of the game. Before you play, you think that opportunity is a gift from the gods; afterwards you feel mortified as you remember everything you might have done but didn't. That was certainly the case with Messi: the night before he was too nervous to sleep and the morning after he regretted not scoring when a good chance came his way. Nevertheless, not long ago I watched that game again and, with hindsight and what I've learned over the years, I quickly realised that the slight lad in the baggy shirt did inject a bit of life, if nothing spectacular, into what was a rather tedious night in Portugal, a country hardly famous for generating thrills. To the point that I wonder what might have happened if he had played longer, even from the kick-off.

As most of the first-team players were with their national squads that afternoon, Frank Rijkaard selected a rather random line-up. Jorquera in goal, Oleguer, Márquez, Navarro, Gabri, Xavi and Luis Enrique were the famous names; the rest of the players came from junior teams. The second half saw the usual round of substitutions you get in a friendly – everyone must get a chance to play – and finally the 74th minute came, the founding moment, the Alpha, the golden baptism, the Origin: Messi took his first paces after jumping onto the pitch to replace Fernando Navarro. He wore the number 14 on his back, which was a real Cruyffian premonition. As he walked towards the area of the pitch his manager had assigned him, the Portuguese TV pundit commented: "In Catalonia they say he reminds them of Maradona."

Such a statement now seems reasonable enough, even predictable, but at the time it must have sounded quite outrageous. Messi was sixteen years, four months and 23 days old. He was the third-youngest player to make his debut in the first team, after Haruna Babangida – whom van Gaal had given his debut at the age of fifteen years, nine months and eleven days – and the legendary striker, Paulino Alcántara – who scored three goals on his debut in February 1929, when he was just fifteen years, four months and eighteen days old.

This record – one of many in Messi's career – perhaps overshadows other more striking aspects of that debut. As if the past insisted on playing tricks with the present, Porto's coach at the time was José Mourinho, and Luis Enrique, Barça's captain for the day, was playing as centre forward. Messi occupied a midfield position – or the "playmaker" role, as he liked to say – and in the 80th minute he received a long, raking pass from Luis Enrique which he almost converted into a goal. A few minutes later he won the ball from the goalkeeper and looked set to score, but decided to pass to a team-mate and the move didn't come off. One could say that Messi made the most of his twenty minutes and was always in on the action, hassling and dangerous. The next morning, the "One by One" section of the *Mundo Deportivo* report gave him three stars, described him as "skilful" and said: "He played like Ronaldinho. His boots could have scored two goals."

That day several other young prospects from the Miniestadi, the Barcelona second-team ground, made their debut with Messi and they were all seeking their moment in the limelight. There was Oriol Riera, who now scores goals for the Wanderers in Sydney; Tiago Calvano, a Brazilian who played for Barça B and has since played in Germany, Switzerland, Australia and the United States; Manel Expósito, another rolling stone, who also went to Australia and has now retired after having played in the Belgian second division; and Jordi Gómez, a youngster like Messi, who soon went to England, then Bulgaria and today plays for Omonia Nicosia, Cyprus. They're all around 30 now and have had less remarkable careers than Messi, but you can bet they remember the afternoon when they made their first-team debuts. "Did I ever tell you about the day Messi and I first played for Barça?" they'll ask, knowing they'll have your attention for the next ten minutes.

2

A YOUNG KID

ABOVE ALL ELSE, EVERY PROFESSIONAL FOOTBALLER starts out as a young kid knocking a ball about. A young kid who wants to shoot at something. They often don't even need an opponent – a wall is enough, or some kind of goal, or simply the desire to boot a ball. Leo Messi was fortunate to have two older brothers – Rodrigo and Matías – and three cousins he used to play mini-matches with, what the Argentines call "*un picadito*", "a kick-about". They'd often come together on a Sunday at their maternal grandmother Celia's, and play morning and afternoon. They all lived in the same district of Rosario and they all followed the same path: first, when they were very young, they played for Grandoli FC, near their house, and then moved on to Newell's Old Boys.

Sometimes, when they criticise Messi's role in the Argentinian national team, the most fundamentalist of fans complain that he didn't learn his football on the dirt track or wasteland of his neighbourhood – or *potrero*, as they call it, the "dusty-field" – but rather *de villa*, that is, on the asphalt, city-style. They've got it wrong. It's true that by the age of five Messi immediately found himself in a club that allowed him to play at a more sustained pace in seven-a-side games, but like all young kids he used every moment he could to play football. One of his teachers remembers how he'd always come along the street to school with a football at his feet. And Jorge Valdano's memories counter the prejudice against city football. Born in Las Parejas, a slum area near Rosario, Valdano also went through his first paces as a player for Newell's, and in an interview he once defined his footballing youth like this: "I walked out of my house and straight onto a thousand square kilometres of football pitch; pampas broken up only by the odd cow or tree, everything else was the pitch."

The world seen as an infinite football pitch. It's an image of freedom to spark our imagination. How often have we heard stories of Brazilian, Colombian or

Argentinian footballers from poor backgrounds, who forged themselves on streets, on beaches, playing barefoot in a *favela*, with a half-deflated ball? It is a mythical image because it appeals to our own childhood and our nostalgia for football without the paraphernalia of the professional sport today. Little games of two against two. Three against three. A goal mouth made from a couple of jumpers.

Perhaps, in contrast, what surprises us most about Messi are the videos from when he was starting out. It's as if everything had been pre-scripted. He belongs to a generation that was filmed on video, so we don't have to imagine how he played as a kid, as we can see him at five, about to turn six, on a dirt pitch in his neighbourhood in Grandoli, and what we see is already spectacular. What I'm going to recount now will make you want to rush to YouTube: Messi is one of the smallest in the team, but he's already wearing the number 10 on his back. Perhaps that's down to his father or perhaps a perceptive coach. When the ball rolls, all the kids run after it, there's barely any organisation or defence – they all want to shoot, whatever it takes. They run without any kind of rhythm and stop when they're tired. They're only five or six years old, what do you expect? However, there is one kid among them who still does what they do, but at the same time is different. He is clever, his moves work out. He goes after the ball and when he's got it, he won't let it go. They can only stop him by fouling him. Otherwise, he runs, dribbles, nutmegs and shoots at goal. The other team restarts from the centre spot: he robs them of the ball and makes another run for a goal. He celebrates for a second and then returns to his half, concentrating again, his arms tight by his side. Let's get back on the attack.

Such is the prehistory of the Messi we know. There are parents who film their children's birthday parties or seaside holidays, and there are others who film their kids playing football.

As Messi developed into the star he now is, more and more people who have met him have shared their memories. Like the Méndez family, for example, in Lima, who still have the first shirt Messi the footballer ever gave anyone. It was a Newell's shirt, black and red. The first time Messi left his country, he went to Peru to play in La Amistad international tournament and lodged in the Méndez family's home. The first night they gave him grilled chicken that was too spicy, and he fell ill. The next morning it looked as if he'd not be able to play, but at the last minute he drank some soda and recovered. That's the kind of detail people remember. They won the first game 10-0 and he scored eight goals. You can find pictures on YouTube of that tournament, which Newell's went on to win. It's four years since he started playing and he's now nine. He's still the shortest player in the side, but the game is better organised around him and he's always the one who creates the break. A defender boots the ball into the air. Young Messi brings it down with great control, dribbles past a defender twice his size and shoots at goal. Now he celebrates like an adult, his team-mates throw themselves on top of him, and shout ecstatically, alternating "*olé, olé,olé*" with "Leo, Leo, Leo!".

His arrival in Barcelona, at the age of thirteen, will catapult all these emotions to a different level. One of the most fascinating things about watching videos of him playing for the Barça youth team is that in many ways he's just like he is now. As if he had been born with all that talent, as if he travelled through time with all his qualities intact. He passed, dribbled, shot, swivelled and finished his moves as if he were today's Messi. The real mystery of his career is what all the videos didn't capture: that day in Rosario when he first dribbled, first shot and first celebrated a goal.

In the video of the *potrero* in Grandoli, whenever the five-year-old Messi scores a goal, you can hear the shouts of celebration. There's a moment when he's tearing up the pitch, on the attack, and someone shouts: "Show them, Leo, show them, show them…" as he dodges past the opposition. Perhaps it is the voice of Celia his grandmother. She was the one who took her grandchildren to those training sessions, and she was also the one who persuaded the coach to let him play at such a young age. Celia was the first major influence on him, though she died when Messi was only eleven. Even today, when he scores a goal, he looks up and points to the sky in memory of his grandmother, and it's as if that gesture crosses the time barrier, back into the past, and we are seeing that same young kid from years ago.

3

THAT PAPER SERVIETTE

WE'RE PROBABLY NOT AWARE OF IT, but we are lucky there are so many kinds of serviette. A visit to Amazon soon shows that when it comes to matters of food hygiene, cellulose is employed in a motley range of varieties, of every size and colour, based on the social class of potential purchasers. At one end, there are serviettes made from a single layer of waxed paper, that are folded in zig-zags and used on a Sunday when we enjoy an aperitif (greasy hands), and at the other, there are those with three layers or more, a luxury item that absorbs spillages of juices and sauces, and is born with an ambition to replace the traditional white cotton serviette. As ever, in between, there is a place for the middle class: the light, conventional serviette, with two layers, that comes with a sandwich or croissant, and

37

which has one essential, unique feature: you can write on it with a ballpoint pen.

On this kind of serviette, which doesn't repel ink because of any lavish finish or defect in the paper, people have written mathematical formulae that have changed the course of science; sketched the aerodynamics of a new car; scribbled poetry describing the most rapturous passion; and jotted football tactics for the 4-4-2 formation. Salvador Dalí paid for restaurant dinners by leaving his autograph on a paper serviette, and the jazz musician Xavier Cugat tried to do the same by offering a caricature (though it didn't always work out for him).

Whatever their social class, all serviettes face the same fate: the rubbish bin. Nobody expects a serviette to last more than a day, or be used more than once. It doesn't have a long-lasting life. That's why, when an item survives its immediate use and enters history, it is often framed like a trophy. Right now the most famous serviette in the world is probably the one that facilitated Leo Messi's first contract and linked him for ever – touch wood – to the history of FC Barcelona.

First of all, the basic facts. The serviette contract was signed around midday on 14 December 2000, when Messi was thirteen, and his signature wasn't on it because, at the time, an Argentinian agent by the name of Horacio Gaggioli managed everything for him. The signing took place in the bar of the Pompeia Tennis Club at the foot of Montjuïc, and it is a piece of luck that someone, at some point, decided that the serviettes in the bar should be the middle-class kind. Gaggioli was accompanied by Josep M. Minguella, another football agent, and Charly Rexach, Barça's then sporting director.

This is more or less how it happened. A few weeks earlier, Leo Messi had passed a test in a Barça training session. As I've said, in the videos of the time you can see how that thirteen-year-old boy was the titchiest on the pitch, but he ran, dribbled and shot with a finesse that makes you rub your eyes. Even though the reports sent from Rosario said that Messi was a powerhouse in the making, it was weeks before the notoriously dilatory Rexach watched him play – Rexach only looked after the bigger lads. One day, when Messi and his father's patience was running out and they were about to pack their bags for Argentina, Rexach told the boy to go to a training session. He put him in a team of lads who were two years older; he only needed five minutes to see that Lionel was an uncut diamond. Rexach enthusiastically supported signing him, but the current directors at the club – Joan Gaspart, Anton Parera and Co – weren't keen to give a contract to a boy from Argentina, because that would mean having to pay for his stay, find his father a job and even fund his hormone growth treatment (which was precisely what Argentinian clubs had refused to fork out for).

Time passed and the Messi family back in Argentina were getting impatient again. Then, one morning, Gaggioli met Minguella and Rexach at the tennis club and gave them an ultimatum: it was now or never. "Now, in this place?" Rexach retorted, and, seeing they were so determined, decided to opt for the paper serviette. Quite unawares, he was launching a legendary career, and in some way that humdrum transaction was of a piece with the unique, inimitable way that Messi plays.

Without any notaries present, and without the leaden, formulaic style of contracts, the document affirms:

In Barcelona, on 14 December 2000 and in the presence of Messrs Minguella and Horacio Carles Rexach Sporting Director of FCB it is agreed under their responsibility and despite numerous views to the contrary to contract Lionel Messi the footballer always provided we keep to the sums agreed.

And, underneath that statement, the signatures of all three. The absence of full-stops and commas in the text, and the omission of Horacio Gaggioli's surname, give us an idea of how last-ditch that agreement was, that there was no time to waste. Even so, Rexach, who is a wily old fox, ensured that the agreement was being signed "despite numerous views to the contrary" and "always provided we keep to the sums agreed". He was protecting his back.

The rest is history: that piece of paper was the pass allowing Messi to return to Barcelona in February 2001, and gradually, not without a few setbacks and tears, to adapt and begin to dazzle all the players and coaches with whom he shared a path through the club's lower tiers.

At some point, when it was evident that Messi would be the best footballer of his era, Horacio Gaggioli framed that paper serviette. He later placed it in a safe deposit box in a bank in Barcelona. Every so often it is rumoured that the Barça Museum will put the famous serviette on show, but Horacio Gaggioli, another wily fox, says that is up for negotiation. Perhaps another contract should be drawn up to specify the terms for ceding that paper serviette. Someone should alert Charly Rexach.

4

ADJECTIVES

TWO CHIPPED GOALS: ONE WITH HIS left leg – the better one – and the other, with his right – which isn't bad either. An opportunistic goal, another after making that run we've seen him make so often, when he drags his opponents from the right to the centre, and then yet another goal, placed gently from the edge of the penalty area. Wonderful, extraordinary, unpredictable, brilliant, unique. That was the night Messi scored five goals at the Camp Nou, against Bayer Leverkusen (7 March 2012). The final result was 7-1, with the other two goals coming from novice Cristian Tello – but what we remember is Messi's quintet, a new record in a Champions League game, and the following morning more than one journalist said, yet again, that the Argentine had exhausted their repertoire of adjectives.

It wasn't the first time and wouldn't be the last. I can't recall any footballer who has provoked such a reaction: nobody ever said that Pelé or Maradona or Cruyff or Di Stefano exhausted the dictionary. Maybe it's a sign of our times – where everything must be defined and categorised ad nauseam – but we can also see it as another reason to dub him the best footballer of all time. *The footballer who exhausted the repertoire of adjectives.*

The first time this phenomenon occurred was, as far as I remember, in March 2010, after Barça beat Real Zaragoza in La Romareda in a league match. We won 4-1 and Messi, who was 23 at the time, scored a hat-trick and won a last-minute penalty. Rather than taking the penalty himself, he left it to Ibrahimović. That goal was a balm for Ibra, who'd had a disastrous match – having missed three glaring opportunities – on the end of a bad run without scoring. Someone, then, could have introduced yet another epithet for the Argentine: generous. Or magnanimous. Or giving.

In the post-match press conference Pep Guardiola said: "There are no adjectives left to describe Messi. I've none, I've run out." Over time, this journalistic ploy – to say that the words don't exist – has become simply one more way of praising Messi's great performances.

Clearly, there's not a dearth of adjectives in the dictionary – there never will be – but there are journalists whose vocabulary dries up. In fact, what Messi does is the opposite: he creates language, activates it, awakens our sense of it, our ingenuity, less obvious associations, poetry. We need to put what we see into words; we want to match his performances. It's not just that he makes us dig deep in our memories – or in the dictionary of synonyms – to find superlative words of praise; he forces us to be more intelligent, so we don't repeat ourselves. The Argentinian dailies, for example, are past masters at this. After the 7-1 win over Bayer Leverkusen, the sports daily *Olé* simply ran the headline: "Picasso", with the subtitle: "Football artist". In Honduras the daily *Diez* alluded to the five goals: "Messi's Fifth Symphony". In Catalonia, *9 esportiu* was even more concise: "Alien".

The writer Màrius Serra devoted two articles in *La Vanguardia* to the matter and, just in case someone was short of ideas, he made a list of 584 adjectives in Spanish from *abismal* to *zaragatero* (which means rowdy, fond of shindigs). Another writer, Marc Pastor, in an article on the *Fot-li Pou* website, later coined a new adjective for posterity: *Messian*. Here's his definition:

Messian [21st cent; from the surname Messi, related to Lionel Messi; pron. mess-ee-an] 1. *adj*. Someone who excels at football, who displays a high level of technique, persistency, quality, power in a game, move or goal. 2. by extension. Used of a match, knock-out leg or final which has witnessed a stellar performance by Leo Messi. Examples: "Santos lost the World Club Final to a Messian Barça". "Barça is experiencing a messianly unbeatable stream of games". "Who's *pichichi* in the League? A Messian Luis Suárez".

In April 2010, a month after La Romareda, when his performance was still sending shivers down our spines, Messi scored four goals against Arsenal at the Camp Nou (4-1), a result that sent Barça through to the Champions League Semi-final. At the end of the game, Arsène Wenger said that Messi was "a PlayStation player" – in a way updating Valdano's praise of Romário years ago when he said the Brazilian was "a cartoon player". In both cases, they were trying to say their performances defied logic and seemed closer to fiction than reality.

Not long ago I re-viewed – I'm now speaking like a film critic – a long replay of highlights from that knock-out match against Arsenal. The commentary was in English and, when Messi scored the third goal, the commentators weren't short on adjectives: *brilliant, bold, magical.* In fact, I often like to see games broadcast in English because I feel the pundits are more skilled in describing great feats. Tradition is on their side, of course, but there is also an instinct for description that goes beyond everyday patter. I followed the last league match of 2016, against RCD Espanyol, on beIN SPORTS, a US channel. They have an amazingly eloquent commentator, Ray Hudson, a former Newcastle United player, and a real ace at creating metaphors. Witnessing Messi's display, crowned by a delicate, subtle goal, Hudson yelled ecstatically: "He is unstoppable! He is Harry Houdini and David Blaine! Next stop, Las Vegas! The best on planet Earth. A genius."

5

CRISTIANO RONALDO

MESSI AND CRISTIANO. 10 AND 7. Mention the two names in one breath and automatically someone is reminded of Mozart and Salieri. Secret Agent 007 against Dr No. Coca-Cola and Pepsi. The Beatles and the Rolling Stones. There are many ways to define the rivalry between these two exceptional players, but perhaps we can start with the statistics.

In the 2014-15 season, the first with Luis Enrique as coach, Barça won La Liga with 94 points and scored 110 goals. Real Madrid were second with 92 points and 118 goals. These are stratospheric figures and when you compare them to the other major European leagues, the differences are colossal. Let's take a look. In Germany Bayern Munich won the Bundesliga with 79 points and 80 goals. In England Chelsea were Premier

League Champions with 87 points and 73 goals. In Italy Juventus won the *scudetto* with 87 points and 72 goals. I know this is only data, and that the game is something else, but it's not hard to work out that it's Leo Messi and Cristiano Ronaldo who make the difference. And more precisely the personal rivalry between the two of them. That season Cristiano was top scorer with 48 goals (ten from penalties) and Messi scored 43 (five from penalties). Without the goals of either, Barça and Real Madrid would still have recorded championship-winning figures in any other league, and maybe even in Spain.

Such stats are the functionary prose of football and, though boring and impersonal, are often revealing. Please forgive me if I quote a few more from the 2014-15 season. Barça were the team that made the most passes during the season (22,114) and Real Madrid came second (17,684). Messi was third in terms of passes by a single player, behind Roberto Trashorras and Toni Kroos, and he was also top for assists: he made eighteen and Cristiano sixteen.

There's no doubt that the struggle between Messi and Cristiano has defined the last few years in La Liga and, even more so, the FC Barcelona–Real Madrid rivalry. Between 2010 and 2013, while José Mourinho lorded it as coach of the *Merengues*, with his rude, defiant style, the duel spread to the benches – for two seasons with Pep Guardiola and Tito Vilanova, and then with Vilanova on his own. Looking back at those years, I recall the acrimony and the unpleasant atmosphere, created by unsporting gestures and accusations – Mourinho's finger in Tito's eye, Pepe's bloodthirsty tactics whenever he was playing against Barça – but also the superior quality of the play, where errors cost dear. And that's the only way to explain seasons of 100 points, or the fact that Messi won the *Pichichi* trophy one year with 50 goals. That's out of this world – 50 goals!

From the perspective of a *barcelonista*, we were the goodies and they were the baddies. What's more, Guardiola and Tito Vilanova represented models of good taste and behaviour, of footballing ideals that seemed to rile Mourinho more by the week. While Guardiola never disputed a referee's decisions, Mourinho often distorted and criticised them to justify defeats, especially if they came against Barça. In defeat, others were always to blame; victorious, he was the cause of success. A Hollywood scriptwriter couldn't have created a better seductive tyrant. Real Madrid fans defended his histrionics by saying that life is a risky business, that hoodlums are always more interesting than heroes, that – as Mae West said – good girls go to heaven, bad girls go everywhere. They liked the role of the anti-hero, it gave them a rabid pride in winning against an unjust world, proof of that pedigree they prize so highly in Madrid. They didn't notice that suddenly, overnight, they had developed a victim mentality and their individuality was defined by comparison to their rivals. The sporting press, with its ability to encapsulate states of mind, dubbed it *barcelonitis*.

When I revisit those years, with the advantage of hindsight, two details stand out. The first is that Cristiano Ronaldo undoubtedly improved under Mourinho, who shaped his desire to win, but also encouraged his petulance, personal vanity and lack of any sense of the ridiculous. The second is that Cristiano Ronaldo came to Real Madrid as the antidote to Messi.

The tendency to compare them, the need to stoke their rivalry, puts them on the same level, but the fact is that Leo Messi – who is two and half years younger than the Portuguese player – was already outstanding. In a word, Messi would always have been Messi. He would have scored goals and beaten records and won Golden Shoes and Ballons d'Or. Cristiano, on the other hand, is more Cristiano thanks to Messi. That's the big difference.

An important ingredient in this rivalry has to do with records and individual prizes like the Ballon d'Or. They are drawn at the moment, with five a-piece, but right now, at the age of 33 and with a game that is increasingly imprecise and less dynamic, it seems unlikely that Cristiano Ronaldo could win another. His transfer to Juventus in Turin in the summer of 2018, to a first-rate league like the Italian one, which is slower and less physical, will allow him to strengthen his transformation into a penalty-box striker, at once more static and more self-centred. Moreover, he is sure to benefit from the glamour surrounding a club like the *Vecchia Signora*, from Italian high society – perfumes, fashion, beauty – and one of the most alluring aspects of the future will be to see how he manages the final years of his career, not to mention his retirement. Will he be the Gloria Swanson of the football pitch, always wanting to be in the spotlight, unable to accept his wrinkles and jealous of other people's success? Or will he try to mirror David Beckham's career and see the catwalk as a continuation of the tunnel from the dressing room. Nobody can deny Cristiano Ronaldo's extraordinary qualities as a footballer – his power, dedication, tenacity and drive – which in another era would have put him at the top of everything for years. With Messi, he still remains at the pinnacle, but always two or three steps below, also waiting to see how new players – the likes of Neymar, Mbappé, Hazard, Coutinho, Pogba, de Bruyne, Salah and Kane – will finally replace them in the fight for the Ballon d'Or.

Another thing is the image he will bequeath to footballing memory. Cristiano's goals have almost always been solitary displays, selfies for private recall. We've all seen him lose his temper when he's not passed the ball, or complain about the lack of commitment of his team-mates after a defeat, or celebrate his own goals, as if football was a solo sport or, worse, a struggle to survive in the style of *The Hunger Games*. His personality thrives on this kind of individual challenge: the muscles, hysterical shouts and nervous tears. With Barça on the other hand, Messi has always followed the ethos of the team, being part of an awesome unit – and he always made sure he appeared in photos with other forwards, whether Ronaldinho, Henry, Suárez or Neymar.

Anyway, although I really don't like prophecies, and even less so in football, I'll leave you with this rather straightforward one: in the distant future, when Cristiano Ronaldo retires, Messi will continue re-inventing himself and scoring goals for a good few years. And let's hope for FC Barcelona.

6

SACRIFICE

THE PASSAGE OF TIME MAGNIFIES LEGENDS and wraps them in an aura of mystery. Gradually facts merge with fiction and it transpires that half of Barcelona went to the Beatles concert in the Monumental theatre in 1965, or that eighteen fingers from the hands of St Lorenzo have been preserved. If today the Messi myth is already planetary, and his statistics seem superhuman, we can't even imagine what will happen in 50 years when the deeds of the best player in history are remembered – because in the meantime it is very unlikely someone similar will emerge. I wouldn't be at all surprised if it is claimed one day that Messi was essentially an Aztec or Mayan or at the very least a pre-Columbian god, and that every year he demanded a forfeit to keep playing for Barça: the sacrifice of a forward at the end of the season.

I don't know if the image going around my head comes from *Tintin and the Temple of the Sun*, or from reading Hernán Cortés's letters, or from the Mel Gibson film, *Apocalypto*. Either way, as I see it, it is a metaphorical sacrifice, naturally, like an offering to the round god of football, as Mexican writer Juan Villoro put it, but the years go by, and the list of victims lengthens...

In the summer of 2008, when Pep Guardiola was promoted to become Barça's coach, replacing Frank Rijkaard, he decided that two of the team's (waning) stars, Ronaldinho and Deco, should have a change of scene. Eto'o looked as if he was about to follow them out, but lasted another season. That season Barça won a trio of trophies, Eto'o scored 36 goals, a great tally, and even scored in the Champions League Final in Rome, when they beat Manchester United 2-0. Nevertheless, the following season the club forced him to transfer to Inter Milan. His place in the forward line was taken by Ibrahimović.

Eto'o was therefore the first forward to lose the privilege of playing alongside Leo Messi. Over the next few months it became clear that playing the towering Ibra – with that moody temperament of his – next to the titch wasn't working and in the summer he was invited to depart to AC Milan on loan. He never returned. That failure, however, did little damage to Guardiola, who in Ibra's view had become "the philosopher" (uttered in a resentful tone). Years later, when he was asked to choose the best eleven of all time, Ibra placed himself alongside Messi and said with a laugh: "Messi is a genius, and I am god."

In 2010 another forward left with Ibrahimović: Thierry Henry. With his light, quick, glittering style, like a Nijinski of the penalty area, he had hit it off with Messi, but was now too old to stand the stress of European competitions, so he went to the States. Ever since, each pre-season period can be seen as a time for sacrifice to the pre-Columbian deity wearing the number 10. The time would come for Bojan Krkić (2011), David Villa (2013), Alexis Sánchez (2014), Pedro (2015), Munir (2016) and Alcácer (2018). We could add a few secondary players who came and went, like Jeffrén, Afellay, Cuenca, Tello, Sandro and Deulofeu – young, often home-grown players, who would be released on loan to another club, and return only to leave after a few months as if their mission was to satisfy Messi's ritual needs.

But why does the list of departing forwards increase? Maybe it's difficult to play next to Messi? Or too demanding? I'd say it was quite the opposite: Messi makes it easy, gives a lot, assists. But he also insists on a leading role that not everyone can tolerate. Of course, individual rapport must be a factor, but it would be wrong to think that Messi only develops rapport and plays well with friends, as is the case now with Luis Suárez (long may it last!). It's rather the reverse: connectivity on the pitch, as with Dani Alves for many years, and more recently with Jordi Alba, might make us think that they would inevitably become friends, almost out of gratitude. But, let's face it, players' private lives are often much simpler than the intrigues spawned by their fans' imagination.

In an article in *El Periódico*, Emilio Pérez de Rozas recalled that, when Chilean Alexis Sánchez came to Barça in August 2011, he expressed his gratitude to Andoni Zubizarreta, then sporting director, for bringing him "to the only club where I could win the Golden Shoe and Ballon d'Or". Alexis was 22, a year younger than Messi, and had excelled in Italy and at the World Cup in South Africa, but he had yet to win anything. Zubi replied – I imagine in that wise, calm tone that never raises any hackles – "Look, Alexis, while the titch stays here, it will be extremely difficult for you to win the Ballon d'Or, let alone the Golden Shoe." Alexis lasted three seasons and then left in search of more goals and more prominence in England, but he has yet to win the Ballon d'Or.

Perhaps we should see the sacrifice of the 2017-18 season more as a case of self-immolation. It would be difficult to imagine, even in the goriest comic book, or Guillermo del Toro horror film, that Neymar's departure was engineered to keep Leo Messi happy. On the contrary: the signings of Luis Suárez and Neymar to play alongside Messi saw the creation of a trident that was extraordinarily beautiful and effective. It seems more likely that Neymar learned his lesson and, with his multi-million flight to Paris Saint-Germain, wished to become another of those gods that demand sacrifices (watch out, Cavani). As for Barça's forward line, for the moment it looks as if the Brazilian's replacement, Ousmane Dembélé, has won the trust of the fans and coach Ernesto Valverde. The tall, lean youngster, a shy, withdrawn millennial, was an expensive signing, but his good performances promise a future in the team. Philippe Coutinho, however, arrived in the shadow of Dembélé, and with the stigma of being the most expensive signing in Barça's history. After one and a half seasons he hasn't succeeded in adapting to the team's footballing style and his performances are tinged by a sadness that verges on the metaphysical. His game requires patience, and Valverde has given him that, but fans have started to look questioningly at him and it wouldn't surprise me if he ended up mounting the sacrificial altar.

7

BEFORE AND AFTER

Diego Armando Maradona was unique in the way he occupied the frontier between sport and spectacle and could turn a pre-match warm-up into entertainment. Sometimes the choreography of his warm-up displays with the Argentinian national team or with Naples was a cross between a circus and an aerobics routine. *El Pelusa* ("The Fluff") would play to the rhythm of a song blaring from the stadium loudspeakers – look for the video with the catchy "Live is Life" by Opus – and even though his boots weren't properly laced, Maradona danced with the ball and dinked with his legs, head and shoulder-blade. Meanwhile he kept his eyes trained on the terraces and once even asked the public to keep time by clapping. I don't know whether that was effective physically but I'm sure it brought people to the stadium early.

Whenever I go to see Barça at the Camp Nou, I try to get there early so I don't miss the players warming up. And this is another of the virtues of Messi and his team-mates in this golden age; as well as the game, I am interested in everything that happens around them before and after the 90 minutes. How they decide their passes, how they joke around as they play a *rondo*, that piggy-in-the-middle with the ball, how they stretch their bodies. In warm-ups, as in training sessions, you see fantastic goals that would go down in history if scored in a match, and yet they are only celebrated by a few attentive fans in the run-up to kick-off.

Messi is like a commercial rep showing you his catalogue of goods that he will then sell you during the game, and sometimes there are spectacular moments. One afternoon at the Camp Nou, for example, I saw Messi and Alves pass the ball to each other over 30 or 40 metres. One was near the corner and the other near the halfway line. One kicked the ball and the other stopped it with his chest, controlled it, dinked it a couple of times and then kicked it back; his team-mate received it, trying to ensure it didn't touch the ground, and then the same over again. The exchange lasted a good long while, ten or twelve passes, and the fans in the ground gradually noticed and watched them, hypnotised. The fan next to me must have spotted my awestruck novice's face and, with the proverbial sang-froid of a long-time club member who's seen it all before, commented: "So what? They do that every week."

Every aspect of a game is there to be enjoyed, and I reckon that television should exploit this vein to the full. Show the before and after, as far as the limits of privacy allow. I don't mean cameras need to enter dressing rooms, but it would be a good idea if, rather than going straight to the adverts after the game, they lingered for longer on those final moments. I like to see the players' reactions – sweating, exhausted, lost in thought, elated or sad – and when they congratulate each other and head to the dressing rooms. I like to see, for example, who they swap shirts with. The look of admiration on opponents' faces when they approach Messi and ask him for that favour (one has that privilege at the end of the first half and another at the final whistle). Don't we watch the whole ceremony after a final, the winners and losers waiting for the cup to be presented, followed by all the celebrations? Well, I'd like to be able to do that after every match, even if for only five minutes. Call me a nerd, if you like, but I believe that this kind of dead time – not to mention the fifteen minutes of half-time in the dressing room – contains lots of information about the game itself: these are the footnotes, coda and credits. What literary theorists call the paratexts: everything that complements the main contents of the game, just like the post-match press conference with the coach and the statements from players.

In a way I am arguing that all football fans are voyeurs and would like to spy on the lives of our idols a tad more after the match. To be flies on the wall, if only for ten minutes. It has all changed a lot and become much more professional, but I remember years ago when I was a kid, sports reporters got us closer to the players. During the pre-season, for example, the sporting press published the schedule for each day's training session – which always took place in Holland back then. They'd tell us how the players were allocated two to a bedroom, what they did in their spare time, what they had for lunch (and I'd ask my mother to cook me the same).

It has to be said that nowadays social media, particularly Twitter and Instagram, function as that open window and players allow us to spy on their lives from time to time, but it all seems much more calculated and mediated.

Talking of private life, I started this chapter with Maradona and I'll end with him too. One day in 1982, in his first season with Barça, the team drew at home against Sporting de Gijón (1-1). I listened to the game on the radio, most likely Joaquim Maria Puyal commentating on Ràdio Barcelona, and it was quite clear that Maradona and the whole team had played a grey, dull game. More than annoyed by the loss of a point (the difference between a draw and a victory was then one point, not two), I felt bad for the player, and with all the naivete of a small-town kid, I decided to call him and cheer him up. I first called directory enquiries and asked for Diego Armando Maradona's number. The operator didn't seem at all fazed and asked me to wait a few seconds and then, incredibly, gave me his number. I jotted it on a scrap of paper and sat quietly, holding the phone, until I'd plucked up the courage. I dialled the seven numbers. Someone picked up the receiver at the other end. The dialogue went something like this:

"Hello?" said a girl with an Argentinian Spanish accent. She was young and I thought she must be his girlfriend, Claudia.

"Hello, is Diego in?" (Note my familiar touch.)

"Who's calling?"

"Well... a friend. I mean, a fan rather than a friend, a Barça fan."

"Ah, right. El Diego isn't here right now. He's not back."

"OK. Please tell him that I'm right behind him and I'm sure we'll win the league because he is the best."

"Ah, thanks!" And she put the phone down.

For a long time I thought her gratitude was sincere, that it must have been true that *El Diego* wasn't back – I imagine from the Camp Nou. In any case, I have never doubted that on that evening I managed to slip into the Maradona clan's home via the telephone wire. I didn't say a word to my school-mates; they would never have believed me.

8

PENALTIES

THERE IS A SELECT CLUB – or maybe it's a secret society – that enrols all the goalkeepers who have saved a Messi penalty. I imagine they meet once a year in a quiet hotel in Benidorm, say, welcome the new members to the club – every season Messi misses the odd penalty – and swap information about the Argentine's latest tendencies. Whether he now fires more to the left, how to keep out *la paradinha* (taken with a "little stop" at the end of the run up), whether there are any magic words to upset him just before he shoots. Galician Diego López deserves to be the president of this select club, the only goalkeeper who has stopped two Messi penalties. And both in Copa del Rey matches. One when he was Villarreal goalkeeper in January 2008 and another ten years later when he was playing for

Espanyol, in January 2018. Vice-president should be Rubén, another Galician who plays for Deportivo de la Coruña and has also seen Messi shoot and miss two penalties on his goal: the first he saved and the second Messi fired into the clouds, to use the usual metaphor.

True enough, penalties are Messi's Achilles heel, but we shouldn't be too anxious because even this weakness has its logic. His figures are slightly below those of other goalscorers, but that shocks us only because we're not used to it; we'd expect him to score every one. So far (April 2019), Messi has taken 105 penalties in competitive games with Barcelona and the national team and missed 24 – that is, almost a quarter. This has two possible explanations – one physical and the other more psychological and creative.

The physical one is simple: according to a study made by *La Vanguardia*, half of the goalkeepers who have saved one of his penalties are over 1.90 metres tall. Seen from the penalty spot, from his 1.70 metres, they are giants who stretch out their arms, dive and fly, easily covering the goalmouth from one post to the other. However, that's an optical illusion, and every Goliath has his David. Besides, Messi often directs the ball to the most surprising places. And if we review all his missed penalties we'll see that he can be resourceful even when he misses. He has missed to the right and the left; he has shot too softly or too hard; the keeper has predicted his aim, he has slipped when he was about to shoot, he has hit the bar and, on three occasions, has collected the rebound from the goalie and scored anyway.

The other, emotional explanation makes a lot more sense: Messi misses penalties because scoring them is too easy. Well, there you are, I've said it! It's not hard to intuit that the absence of a big challenge, the defencelessness of the goalie standing before him, and even the routine nature of scoring a penalty all go against him. When he shoots from a free kick, at least there is a wall. What's more, a penalty is an opportunity to think. Too many options, too many alternatives. That lengthy pause between the moment the referee points to the fateful spot and Messi places the ball, faces the goalie and has to shoot must be torture, what with so many ideas spinning around his head – I mean, he is a footballer used to deciding what to do in tenths of a second, almost exclusively driven by intuition.

Years ago, when Maradona went back to play in the Argentinian league, after his adventures in Europe, he missed five penalties on the trot. That must be some pressure, Sunday after Sunday.

Even though being the penalty taker is a way of being the team's standard bearer (and of boosting one's goal tally), now and then Messi does give that honour to his team-mates. It is a form of altruism that at the same time frees him from that *embarras du choix* of the penalty kick. We have seen him hand over penalties to Luis Suárez, to Neymar, and, as we've already mentioned, to Ibrahimović in Zaragoza.

So far the most painful penalty Messi has missed – and the most costly – must be the one he took for Argentina in the Copa América Final, in June 2016, against Chile. The game and extra time had finished goalless and he was the player charged with opening the penalty shoot-out for his team. Seconds earlier, Arturo Vidal had missed the first one for Chile and now Messi had the chance to set Argentina on the path to victory – but he sent the ball into the stratosphere, to use another common image. Bravo, the Chilean keeper, saved another, from Biglia, and Chile won the cup.

At the other extreme, Messi must be one of the few players who has voluntarily missed a penalty, and it must have been his sweetest miss from the spot. On 14

February 2016, St Valentine's Day, in a match against Celta de Vigo, when Barça were winning 3-1, the famous penalty that would be seen around the world was taken. I've just watched it again on YouTube. Before he shoots, Messi and his colleagues exchange quick glances. He walks up to the ball and, instead of hitting it hard, taps it to his right, a timid, unexpected pass, apparently aimed at Neymar, but Suárez gets there first and scores the goal. Commentators across the world rubbed their eyes and described that move as if they'd just seen a Martian. It is an abstract penalty, a meta-penalty. Ray Hudson, the amazing commentator we met earlier in this book, yelped and said: "What we have seen here is totally Shakespearian! But Shakespeare got it wrong: it wasn't *King Lear*, it is *King Leo*!"

Messi is so good that, now and then, he has the virtue of searching tradition and recreating mythical moves from the history of football. In this case, there is a clear echo in our minds of the penalty that Johan Cruyff invented in December 1982, playing for Ajax. In that original version, Cruyff passes to the left, a team-mate plays a one-two back and Cruyff himself scores. Messi's decision must have been a homage to Cruyff: the day before, the Dutchman had confirmed on his webpage that he was fighting lung cancer, and for the moment was winning the game. Cruyff died several weeks later, on 24 March, but I am sure that Messi penalty gave him a few more breaths of life.

9

THE 21ˢᵗ CENTURY

LITERATURE AND FOOTBALL SHARE FEW THINGS in common, but there is one that unites them: the difficult task of correctly predicting writers and players who will shape the future. Glance at poetry anthologies of promising new voices, or articles that have just discovered the new Nabokov, Rodoreda or Bolaño, and it is usually the case that ten years later reality has belied so much enthusiasm. The same happens with football analysts and talent-spotters: every week they discover a new Cruyff or Maradona, and I'm sure there are parents of the current Barça youth teams who think their son will be the new Xavi, Puyol or Valdés. (I ought to add that, for now at least, I've not heard of anyone who's seriously spotted "the new Messi", perhaps because he is so extraordinarily good it would be absurd to suggest *anyone* can play like him, and in any case we should always remember Picasso's quip: "Blessed be my imitators, for they shall inherit my faults.")

We also know that most literary critics and football analysts have cultivated their clinical eye through theoretical observation, and rarely excelled physically in the art they study with such devotion – and shirts versus skins kickabouts, or writing occasional verse for a friend's retirement don't count. However, from time to time, there is an exceptional intellect who, based on personal experience, dares to make a prediction and gets it right. I am thinking, for example, of the great Helenio Herrera, A.K.A. the Magician, contradictory myth, changing-room psychologist and visionary of modern football. In 1979, when Maradona was nineteen and beginning to shine for Argentinos Juniors, but had yet to win anything, H.H. gave an interview to the sporting magazine *El Gráfico*, and they asked him what the footballer of the future would be like. He replied, "The footballer of the 21st century will be very like Maradona. Short but very athletic, with that magic that computers and Maradona possess". He couldn't possibly have known, but he was defining Messi.

Five years later, in 1984, shortly before he died, the

writer Italo Calvino wrote a series of lectures that he
had planned to deliver at Harvard University, and that
were published in English under the title *Six Memos
for the Next Millennium*. Calvino outlined five concepts
which he believed would define art and literature in the
21st century and which artists and critics should take
into account: lightness, quickness, exactitude, visibility
and multiplicity. Quite unawares, he too was speaking
of Leo Messi.

Lightness

Calvino defends and demands of artists a series of
qualities that Messi exploits with that mixture of intuition and awareness, talent and experience that only
the best footballers have. Messi was already light when
he was a kid, too much so, in fact, and growth hormone treatment provided him with exactly the point
of gravity he needed. Moreover, that physical lightness
has also become mental – or spiritual, if you prefer –
as the years have passed and he has enjoyed so much
success. Calvino focuses above all on the hero Perseus,
"who flies on winged sandals",* and, inspired by his

---

* All the quotations are from Geoffrey Brock's new translation, *Six
Memos for the Next Millennium*, Penguin Modern Classics, 2016.

attitude, recalls a series of writers who create that sense of agility – from Lucretius, who seems to want to "prevent the weight of matter from crushing us", to Shakespeare when he has Prospero say "we are such stuff as dreams are made on". All those references are reflected, I think, in the ease with which Messi swerves between defenders, as if his feet weren't touching the ground. But if I had to choose the moment that best illustrates his lightness it must be the goal he scored in the Champions League Final in Rome against Manchester United, on 27 May 2009. Xavi has the ball on the right of the halfway line, looks for a pass and sees Messi pop up between two defenders on the edge of the penalty area. That deep-lying position shows he is expecting a cross, and Xavi reacts instantly, delivering a speedy, accurate ball into the box. Messi runs and suddenly jumps, rises above the defender (Ferdinand, who is 1.89 metres tall) and hovers for the amount of time needed to head the ball and send it over the goalkeeper (van der Sar, who is 1.97 metres tall). His body arches back so he can get a better contact on the cross, and, if it weren't for the fact that his header is so precise as to send the ball over the keeper – and it is a goal, the most earth-bound thing in the world – you'd say that Messi might have risen like a helium balloon, light and weightless, into the sky.

Quickness

In the hands of Italo Calvino, quickness is above all "the relationship between physical and mental speed". However, quickness also requires the art of pausing, of knowing when to stop occasionally to ensure effectiveness of speed. Quoting a story from Boccaccio's *Decameron*, Calvino observes "that even proper style requires a readiness to adapt, a nimbleness of expression and thought". Sometimes, Messi's quickness is mere illusion. He isn't the quickest player, or the one who runs the most in a game, but he certainly is one of the best when it comes to adapting his pace to what he wants to achieve. Moreover, he is one of the swiftest with the ball at his feet, and when getting rid of it, never dallying, releasing it to the right spot. His brain works so quickly it often seems a reflex action, an instinctive, inevitable act, which is why he rarely lingers frivolously. When he's dribbling, for instance, if one step over is enough, he won't do two (a critical dig aimed at Cristiano Ronaldo's baroque interludes).

There are many examples of this quickness applied

to his game, but my favourite is the goal he scored on 30 May 2015, in the Copa del Rey Final against Athletic Bilbao, which is one of his best ever. His predatory nature the second he scents the chance to score, his swivelling legs as he swerves past three opponents in a second, his pauses to choose his path to goal and the speed with which he shoots when he sees a gap: everything combines to create a miraculous goal.

Such beauty and transcendence mean that many fans rate it as one of the best ten goals ever. The daily *Sport* analysed the move scientifically and wrote that the whole thing took 11.4 seconds and Messi ran 55 metres. When he shoots, he does so with such precision through the only possible avenue. If he had placed it 1.5 millimetres more to the right or left, the goalkeeper would have stopped the ball or it would have hit the post.

Exactitude

Quickness, then, is even more effective when accompanied by exactitude. In this case, however, Calvino emphasises that it is an artistic wager in favour of "the evocation of sharp, memorable images" and "a language that is as precise as possible", against a "terrible plague" that encourages casual, loose, ill-conceived writing. The precision with which Messi plays is also challenging, and should serve as an example against the background noise impoverishing football: the fouls, time-wasting, diving, shocking defending and the egoism of forwards. Messi never dives in the penalty box, is never tempted by theatrical outbursts and doesn't resort to frills to prettify his game. Consequently, he doesn't like coaches who speculate about results, or arbitrary referees who have no clear criteria as regards fouls or who encourage play acting.

Calvino quotes a text by Paul Valéry where he defines the creative impulse of Edgar Allen Poe, and it could easily be a description of Messi's football: "the demon of lucidity, the genius of analysis and the inventor of the most novel and seductive combinations of logic and imagination."

Visibility

When predicting what a 21st-century footballer might look like, Helenio Herrera said he would have the magic that computers possess, which makes me think of the numerous occasions someone has remarked that Messi's football is like a video game. It's very likely that

H.H., with the ideas people had of computers in 1979, was referring to the mystery of processing information with such inhuman, magical complexity, and video game fans see in Messi a way of playing and a rhythm and array of resources that only seem feasible in virtual reality, and not on the turf of an actual football pitch. Italo Calvino defines visibility as the knack of imagining something that's impossible, something that has never existed before. We live in an era where images force themselves upon us and overwhelm us with their excesses. In the days of László Kubala or Sir Stanley Matthews, footballers rarely saw the goals they scored, let alone the goals of their opponents. The most they could do was remember them and refresh their memories with the help of newspaper reports and photos. And the same went for spectators: if you weren't in the ground, radio commentaries and the next morning's newspaper reports and graphics were the main sources, if not the only ones, if you wanted to reimagine the moves.

Today it is quite the opposite. We watch games live and we see the key moves repeated from every angle, in slow motion, and accompanied by expert comment. The next morning we can revisit them on the internet, compare them to other moves in the past and analyse them. And footballers do this too: when you are creative, your game often comes not from pure imagination but from the repeated viewing of what you have already seen. We even see it in the way little kids play in the street or school playground: they try to dribble like Ronaldinho, celebrate goals with a Dani Alves samba or copy Neymar's hairstyle. Not forgetting the coaches, who with their strategies and tactics try to predict what is unpredictable by its very nature...

In this context, Calvino states that visual imagination must be accompanied by an order that gives it meaning – style, in the case of narrators – that is, "a web in which reasoning and verbal expression also impose their logic". Translated to the world of football, it means the ability to invent and find solutions must be controlled by a sense of what is practical: nobody with an ounce of common sense starts making elaborate dummies in his own penalty area or risks a difficult overhead kick (which would be even more spectacular) when a straightforward header is possible.

A good example of this sense of intent is the direct free kick. In his professional career with Barça and the Argentinian national team, Messi has scored 43 goals from direct free kicks (as of April 2019). Most have gone in to the left of the goalkeeper, looking for the top corner, and he's only twice tried to do something tricky: namely, to shoot along the ground and send the ball under the wall. The first time was in an Argentina–Uruguay World Cup qualifier, and immediately it seemed the best, if not the only, option. The second was when Girona played at the Camp Nou as a first-division team on 24 February 2018. Messi took the free kick using the same strategy – and scored. Immediately, all of us Barcelona fans remembered Ronaldinho scoring a goal like that in his glory days. So Messi is a footballer who reinvents the classics. What's more, now, whenever there is a free kick, opposition goalkeepers have to contemplate that possibility, and players in the wall have to ask themselves: what do I do? Do I jump or don't I?

Multiplicity

Even when Messi doesn't play, when he's not in the ground, he plays for Barça. His absence, reasonably enough, isn't as decisive as his presence, but it is natural he should influence the game. If it happens to be one of those rare days when the coach has left him on the bench, the opposing team's players watch him out of the corner of their eyes and fear the moment when he comes on, and that threat, to an extent, conditions their game: maybe it makes them hurry too much to try and decide the match before he appears, or perhaps it is the reverse, he slows them down, quells their desire to attack, so as not to awaken the beast. When Messi isn't on the turf, his team-mates also play differently. There are eleven of them, but they know it's like playing with ten, because *that* number 10 is irreplaceable. Then his absence spurs them on, gives them a different sort of edge. When they have the ball at their feet, they look for him, don't see him, and play on hoping he will appear as if by magic – because he is always there – and they have no choice but to fill the gap he has left.

This presence *in absentia* is also one of the many combinations that give Messi multiplicity. Italo Calvino chooses another Argentine, Jorge Luis Borges, and refers to "the model of a network of possibilities [that] can therefore be condensed into a few pages of a Borges story". And what can be said about a story can also be said about a collective move when in possession of the ball. At another moment in his text, Calvino writes: "The best-loved works, in contrast, arise from the confluence and collision of a multiplicity of interpretive methods, modes of thought and styles of expression." Messi offers the profile of a player who, with every move, explodes into a thousand hues and at the same time condenses the essence of football, all the things that must be done well in the game. Ask fans how Messi plays and you'll get a range of replies. The most accurate will say: "Every way!" Since he started with Rijkaard as a right-winger, via his time with Guardiola as a false 9, the Argentine has tried out various positions, from midfield upwards. Moreover, when necessary, he runs back to defend, retrieves balls and is the first forward to press up the field. Messi spreads himself across the pitch, scores goals and assists, orchestrates moves and passes. One day long ago he learned that he didn't have to make every move from start to finish, but that each pass, each run made by a team-mate offered an alternative. And hope for the future lies in that multiplicity, because he constantly finds the place where he can be useful. The years will go by, the time to retire will approach and, as he moves away from the penalty area because he isn't so decisive there, I am sure he will always find a way to become visible.

10

DIEGO ARMANDO

"Sometimes Maradona was Maradona.
Messi is Maradona every day."
Santiago Segurola

Argentina won their second World Cup on 29
June 1986, when it was held in Mexico. An impetuous,
Dickensian novelist, a lover of coincidences, would doctor the calendar so Messi was born exactly nine months
later, a happy consequence of that happy afternoon.
But he was actually born almost a year later: on 24
June 1987. In any case, we know that nervy, skinny kid
grew up in a country where Diego Armando Maradona
was the mega media star, the name all Argentines could
agree on. The country was experiencing a return to
democracy and much political upheaval. The military

dictatorship had ended and Raúl Alfonsín had been elected as the president, but his plan to restore social harmony was beginning to fracture over the will to call the military to account. Laws of impunity were passed in an attempt to dilute sentences for crimes committed under the dictatorship and sabres were occasionally rattled. Meanwhile, the Madres de la Plaza de Mayo continued to demonstrate and demand justice for the disappeared – and Sting sang "They Dance Alone" and invited the Madres to his concerts so everyone could hear about their tireless struggle.

Maradona was then playing for Naples; he was a distant star. The year after the World Cup he won the *scudetto* and the Coppa Italia, which made him an even more famous footballer. Many already believed he was the best in the world. While Messi was growing up in Rosario, Maradona won another league title in Naples and lost the World Cup Final in Italy with Argentina in 1990, and a few months later tested positive for the first time in a drugs test. He was suspended for fifteen months and didn't play a single competitive game. In 1992 he went to Sevilla for a season, lured by the club's manager, Carlos Bilardo. He wore his hair shoulder length and captained the team from his very first game;

he no longer ran very fast but created assists like an angel and needed no encouragement to shoot. By the end of the season Maradona was almost 33 and his ability was on the decline, but he knew he had one more chance at the World Cup – in the United States in 1994 – and so decided he must play in Argentina again.

He was certainly in a position to choose and get a deal, and he opted for Newell's Old Boys in Rosario. He played his debut game on 7 October 1993 in a friendly against Emelec from Ecuador – a game that finished with a 1-0 victory for Newell's, with a good goal from Maradona, who had had a haircut and looked in better shape. Forty thousand spectators came to the stadium that night to welcome him, and when he scored that goal several rushed onto the pitch to congratulate him. Among the crowd was a six-year-old Messi, accompanied by his father, possibly bored like all kids his age, perhaps sleepy-headed, but undoubtedly fascinated by that character on the pitch. At this point you can be sure the opportunistic novelist would have him jump on the pitch and go hug the Argentinian idol.

Rosario was a good place for Maradona to make his return to football in his country. He avoided the pressure-cooker atmosphere of Buenos Aires, yet at the same time he was playing in a city with a long and distinguished footballing tradition. The main rivalry is between the city's two big teams, Newell's Old Boys and Rosario Central. The fans of Ñuls (the Spanish pronunciation of Newell's) are known as "lepers", and they wear the name with pride. That rebarbative-sounding nickname comes from the 1920s when the two clubs were supposed to play a benefit game for the Lepers Foundation. Rosario Central backed out, perhaps on account of an absurd notion of hygiene, and from then on their rivals insulted them with the epithet of "swine", and the response made "lepers" of the fans of Newell's.

I wonder whether Leo Messi went to that game wearing the lepers' red-and-black shirt. Everyone at home supported Ñuls – except for one brother, Matías, who backed Rosario Central. Leo's father gave him his first shirt when he was one. You can find this kind of detail about his childhood in the excellent biography of Messi by Guillem Balagué (Orion Books, 2013). The house where he lived when he was a kid: Calle Estado de Israel, 525. His parents' ages when he was born: Jorge Messi, 29, and Celia Cuccittini, 27. The names of the teachers who coached him at school. His progress in maths and language at the age of eight, when he started to play football more intensively…

In the end, Maradona's fling with the "lepers" was short-lived. He played only five competitive games, and didn't score a single goal. Using the excuse that he was injured, he walked out and, with no team behind him, prepared for his return to the national selection with a view to the World Cup that summer of 1994, when we now know he again tested positive in a drugs test.

On 21 March in that same year, only two months after Maradona's last game for Newell's, Messi was first contracted to play for the same club. A starting-point. One inevitably imagines what might have happened had Maradona stayed in Rosario. What if, one day, he'd come out of a training session, and someone had mentioned that extraordinary little titch, a unique player, and *El Dios* might have taken twenty minutes of his time to go to the youth training ground and bless the young boy. The range of possibilities is huge; my hunch is that we would all have lost out, Leo most of all – but there's no point going down that path. There's no point because then I start imagining the worst and thinking that maybe we would never have seen him play for Barça.

11

AERODYNAMICS

"Messi is the only player who is quicker with the ball at his feet than without it."

Pep Guardiola

IF MESSI HAD BEEN BORN IN Brazil, he would surely have become Messinho, or even Messizinho, and there are still journalists in Argentina who refer to him by his nickname, *la Pulga* ("the Flea") which is what he was called in his first club, Newell's Old Boys. When he came for his first trials with Barça, on 17 September 2000, Messi was thirteen years old and was less than a metre and a half in height (1.48 metres). In an interview in 2004 on Argentinian television, the player himself said that "the hormone was asleep" – the growth hormone – and, thanks to treatment paid for by FC Barcelona, after five years he was 1.69 metres tall and weighed 67 kilos. Three years later, at 21, he was the 1.70 metres he is now, which is possibly the ideal height for a footballer, especially if he is a winger or midfielder with a light touch. It's almost as if they had given him growth hormones until he reached his ideal height and then stopped.

From time to time, a scientist appears out of nowhere and painstakingly tries to demonstrate what all of us know already: that Messi is the best in the world. You have to admit that data and theory make it sound even more true. In an era dominated by tall, strong footballers, Messi is a miracle of biomechanics who makes the most of his low centre of gravity. In an article on the *Bleacher Report* sports website, Ross Edgely, adventure athlete and sports writer, quoted the *British Journal of Sports Medicine*, stating that "within the field of sports science, elite performance is understood to be the result of both training and genetic factors" – that is, a balance in the eternal nature vs nurture debate. In cases where genetic factors are out of kilter – as in young Messi's case – hours of training can compensate for what's lacking. His dribbling skills, for example, come from exercises he has done from a very early age to overcome his physical disadvantage, and Edgely clarifies further: "footballers with a shorter running stride and lower centre of gravity are able to decelerate quickly, anticipate changes in motion and accelerate quickly." This was the case with Garrincha, one of the most fantastic dribblers of the ball in the history of the game: he was born with crooked legs and, through hours and hours of training, overcame his defect to become supremely skilful.

Thus, at 1.70 metres, give or take a centimetre, Messi joins a line of players who have dominated at dribbling and possession of the ball – partly because they are closer to it. Just to give a few examples: Maradona is 1.65; Romário and Zagallo, 1.67; Xavi, 1.68. The great Garrincha was 1.69, like Alexis Sánchez and Pedro. Raheem Sterling and Jordi Alba, 1.70, Iniesta, I.71. And thereafter players are too tall, at least as far as standards go in the Spanish league and the kind of football played there. In a conversation with Jorge Valdano, Johan Cruyff praised Messi's unique qualities and observed that, in order to be able to decide when to dribble and when to lose his marker, it was essential for him to have team-mates who were one-touch players, like Iniesta and Xavi. "Besides," he said, "he has the huge advantage that he can look them in the eye, because they are his height. Such details make the difference."

Naturally, height isn't everything, and you need a special instinct to extract the right aerodynamics from your body. One of the ways in which Messi excels is in his ability to pause in movement. In the same way that he can accelerate with the ball at his feet, or anticipate a defender's reaction – the step forward, the position of the feet – a hundredth of a second before other players, which often gives him a decisive advantage, he also knows how to control the tempo of a move and include a tiny pause, less than half a second, that allows him to dictate play. It's as if he can bring time to a halt, as if he can reset the move to gain an advantage.

In the world of music, the most commercial producers long for what they call "the money note". That's their name for the musical note that means a pop song will be a big international hit. Sometimes it's a higher or longer note, or even a brief silent beat that holds up the flow of the melody. It's the moment everyone remembers and, whenever you hear that song again, you wait for it. One of the best known is Whitney Houston's song "I Will Always Love You", where the money note comes after 3.10 minutes: the briefest pause, a beat of the drums and then the voice belting out: "And aaaa-yyaaaaay…" And, in his song "Faith", George Michael found that money note when incorporating a silent pause. Sometimes, when I see Messi dummy, move forward and stop (almost slipping expressly on the turf for half a second), I think of that musical strategy: the pause that hypnotises his opponent and gives him the advantage.

Overall, Messi is the most influential player in the Spanish league, but he isn't the one who falls to the ground most often or the most targeted by defenders. In the 2016-17 season Neymar was the most fouled player (126), while Messi was tenth in the table of the afflicted (*only* 79 fouls). The fact is it's very difficult to stop Messi, by fouling him or not. Sometimes, when I review some of his goals that come from open play, I get the impression that his opponents move aside, as if they were scared by the very sight of him, or just want to watch him and see what he will do next. Clearly, that's a mistaken impression. I'm remembering that goal in the Champions League Semi-final against Bayern Munich, the one that made it 2-0 – I mean the one against Boateng. Messi, racing up the pitch, receives a ball outside the area and heads towards goal. He is being marked by Boateng, who leaves the right side free because he knows the right is Messi's bad (or less good) leg. Messi dummies to the left, makes Boateng hesitate for moment, and then cuts him dead by dribbling to the right. Boateng can't physically stand that swerve, he is too tall and heavy, and falls to the ground as if deliberately – a clownish piece of slapstick. Messi then continues unopposed and when Neuer comes out of his goalmouth, he beats him with a delicate chip. I see many defenders who have suffered at the feet of Messi reflected in what happened to Boateng, great players who watch Messi impose his centre of gravity on them: the game is played at his height.

I've said that it's very difficult to foul him, but it's not as if defenders don't try. When they're not left prostrate like poor Boateng, opponents try to destabilise him with their bodies, pushing, chasing, pulling his shirt, but he always gets up, always goes on, gives nothing up as lost. A few years ago, in 2012, the Argentinian writer, Hernán Casciari, who was living in Barcelona at the time, earned a spell of fame with a provocative, moving and beautiful essay: "Messi is a dog". He published it in the magazine *Orsai*, after watching a video called *Messi never dives*. It was a compilation of clips in which his opponents use all manner of fouls and knocks, stamp on him and trip him up to try to stop him, but he always gets up and goes on, obsessively, never complaining. Casciari writes that "Messi's eyes are always focused on the ball, not on the game or the context". As if he were "in transit, hypnotised", with a single objective, getting that ball into the rival goal. Such an attitude, he writes, reminds him of the little dog he had when he was a kid. It would seize a sponge it liked in its teeth and there was no way it would let go. It only had eyes for the sponge. "Messi is a dog," he writes, "Messi is a sick man. It is a rare disease that moves me, because I loved *Totín* and now [Messi] is the last dog-man." We can agree that it's a way-out, rather irreverent comparison, but serves to highlight the pure, animal instinct that often drives Messi when he is playing football.

12

MARADONA

I SOMETIMES WONDER WHEN MARADONA REALISED that Messi was better than he was, if indeed he ever has. (Yes, I know, I'm unashamedly throwing myself in at the deep end.) Was it the day that Leo scored "that Maradona goal" against Getafe? Messi was nineteen at the time and, with a veteran's elan, reproduced quite unconsciously the great goal Maradona scored against England when he was 25. It was as if he was telling him: now I've scored your best goal, I'm rid of all the pressure on my back.

Maradona didn't concede; quite the contrary. As Leo has won more titles and broken more records, Diego has made sure that we know Messi doesn't have the main title that he holds, the most coveted: a World Cup won with Argentina. Over the years, this lacuna (which can still be sorted, let's not forget) has created a memorial of grief that weighs heavily on Messi and his family. Diego himself has never been slow to criticise, for example at one of the national team's lowest ebbs, when they were coached by Basile, *el Coco* ("the Brainbox"), and had to qualify for the 2010 World Cup. After a soporific game which Argentina drew with Peru, Maradona was commenting on a sports channel and said: "Sometimes Messi plays for Messi. He is Messi FC." A nasty jibe, right?

When they broach this issue, most Argentines say you shouldn't make comparisons, that both are exceptional; then they immediately do just that. They can't avoid it. "Messi is a poster, Maradona is a flag," noted Hugo Asch. In the magazine *Jot Down* Patricio Pron wrote that it is an "impossible and undesirable comparison", especially given the country's socio-historical state, and he attempted another kind of description: "We Argentines like Maradona because his excesses, accidents and falls are a reflection of ourselves, or what we'd like to believe: that the possession of talent leads to the damnation of the individual thus gifted, which means it's not worth making the effort." Eduardo Sacheri is another writer who has reflected more straightforwardly, saying, for example, that they can't be compared because with Maradona it's already a "complete works" whereas with Messi it's a "work in progress". Who knows what he still has to offer? Sacheri also writes very insightfully: "It is not Messi's fault if we Argentines are unable to find closure in our mourning over Diego, his retirement, his departure, the undoubted fact that he will never play again."

It may be that this impossibility of closure, as Sacheri puts it, even for Maradona himself, is connected to Messi. People say they have both made an effort to come together, and it's probable that over the years their relationship has even become friendly and relaxed – but it is shot through by Diego's know-it-all attitude and his insistence on handing out advice.

In any case, there is a key moment in their relationship: when Maradona became the national team manager in October 2008, with the mission of leading Argentina to victory in the 2010 World Cup. Aware that he depended on Messi, Maradona listened to him, asked him how he would like to play, and with which team-mates. He made him captain rather than Verón (a move that would have delighted Maradona the player, but perhaps was a responsibility Messi wasn't yet ready for); he made him number 10, a clever enough ploy that was also highly symbolic: it is the number *he* wore, followed by *Burrito* Ortega, Andrés D'Alessandro, Pablo Aimar, Juan Román Riquelme and Verón himself. And that is striking. In an interview Javier Mascherano casually revealed that Maradona saw Messi as a projection of himself on the pitch – "he had become 30 years younger!" says *el Jefecito* – something that makes me think of the latest Woody Allen films, in which he chooses actors to play a role that deep down is himself.

The necessary ingredients were there, but it never worked. Messi didn't feel involved with the team. With Pep Guardiola's Barça he had managed to give the best version of himself, that of playmaker with an absolute freedom of movement. Maradona looked for an Argentinian version of Xavi, Iniesta, or Busquets, but never found them. The figures show that when Maradona was his manager, Messi scored three times in sixteen games. Paltry. He played in the World Cup in South Africa and never had sight of goal; Argentina were eliminated by Germany (4-0) in a catastrophic quarter-final. Spain won that World Cup and I wonder if Messi ever regretted a decision he took years ago in Barcelona. When he was seventeen, the Spanish

Federation had tempted him to play for the *Rojita* in the Under-17 World Cup, as a naturalised Spaniard alongside Cesc and David Silva, among others. However, he chose Argentina.

13

WALKING THE WALK

THERE ARE FEW PLAYERS WHO WALK better in a game than Messi. Some run more, are nimbler, or cover more ground with their strides, but the way Messi walks is unique. Beckenbauer walked through the defence like someone strolling through a garden on his own private property: "*you* can come in, *you* can't." When he wasn't involved in a move, *Mágico* González shuffled through his opponents' area with the insouciance of a *flâneur*. Ibrahimović walks with the majestic air of a long-shanked bird, a flamingo that knows it is being admired. Messi doesn't; Messi walks as if he has lost his keys or something. He seems to keep his eyes on the ground, covering a small area, and at times you think he is working out how far he is from his opponents, whether it's worth getting nearer or not. There are anxious goalies who walk further than Messi in a game, up and down, up and down. If he were another player, I'd feel like asking him to run more, but when it comes to Messi, we know that's unnecessary: he never loses sight of the game and knows how to economise on effort.

Strangely, Messi's walks only worry Barça fans when the team isn't playing well. The year when they were trained by *Tata* Martino, for example, the 2013-14 season, Messi walked more than ever. "He's saving himself for the World Cup," we said, as if to justify his perambulations.

In October 2013, the first year that Pep Guardiola coached Bayern Munich, I visited him in his lair on Sabernerstrasse. Pep showed me the training pitches, the ultra-modern facilities, and we had a coffee in his office which was like a spaceship. That afternoon Guardiola was preparing for that week's Champions League game against Viktoria Pizen from the Czech Republic. He showed me the computer screen where he was watching the last game Viktoria had played in their national league and I soon noticed the image was odd. Then he told me why: his team of assistants recorded opponents' games with a fixed camera that took in the whole pitch. Rather than see the actions of an individual player, he wanted to have a general view of the rival team's movements, the to-and-froing, areas of pressure, the natural flow of each player. Now I remember that and think how I would like to see an entire Barça game from this static perspective – it would be like sitting in that vantage-point in the ground. I would like to concentrate solely on Messi and watch him constantly walking, oblivious to everything happening around him, as he seems to be, and follow his movements and reactions: those seemingly random steps in no particular direction, this way and that, and, suddenly, the whiplash, the chase to latch onto a pass, or his presence spurring on a move, the start of something that will surely be decisive.

In the famous Copa del Rey game against Getafe, for example, with the Maradonian goal. It's wonderful to watch in its entirety, anticipating what will happen in the 29th minute. It's like seeing a favourite film once again, Blake Edwards' *The Party*, say, waiting for the moment when Peter Sellers loses his shoe in the swimming pool. You've seen it lots of times, you know it by heart, but repetition simply increases your pleasure. So then, it's the 29th minute and Messi is playing on the far right, near the halfway line. A couple of minutes ago he came back to defend and sent the ball out for a corner. He's now recovering from the effort. He follows the play from afar. Four steps forward, two steps back; three steps forward, one to the side, two back. He looks up and stiffens when he sees the ball heading his way; he relaxes when his team loses the ball and starts walking again, slowly. Suddenly Xavi gets the ball, comes towards him and he straightens. His expression seems to say "I am here", even though Xavi already knows that is the case. Messi waits. He receives the ball and immediately makes his first feint to move past a player. Another dribble, and another, and so on. Twelve seconds go by, only twelve, before collective lunacy erupts.

There's another strategy I think I would prefer, the opposite of Guardiola's fixed screen, one that allows you to focus on a player and follow him across the pitch. In 2006, video artists Douglas Gordon and Philippe Parreno premiered the film *Zidane: A 21st Century Portrait*. Conceived halfway between a documentary and a work of art, it follows everything Zinedine Zidane does during one match. On 23 April 2005, on the occasion of a Real Madrid–Villareal FC game, the two artists installed seventeen synchronised cameras in the Santiago Bernabeu stadium that followed Zidane during the whole match. Close up, from a distance, sweating, dribbling, running, talking, calling for the ball. Every camera focused on him. In the background, the din from the fans and, now and then, snatches of music from the Scottish band Mogwai. The combined images construct a physical and mental study of that individual, a portrait of the last great player of the twentieth century. Almost at the end of the game, Zidane gets caught up in an altercation, attacks a rival and is sent off, so even in this detail the film communicates football's unpredictable nature.

Sometimes, when I see Messi walking on the pitch, and doing those things that only he can do, I think he deserves a filmed portrait like Zidane's. A work of art in movement; he surely is, and will be, *the* great player of the 21st century. All the cameras following him in one game, probing his enigmatic talent. We'll never know what's going on inside his head while he's playing, but at least we would get a tiny bit closer.

14

RONALDINHO

In the summer of 2004, at the end of July, my stars aligned and *El País* sent me to report on FC Barcelona's tour of Asia. Perhaps, rather than my stars, it was the fact that it coincided with the Olympic Games in Athens – the destination of most sports journalists – and that a colleague broke her leg at the last minute, so Ramon Besa, the newspaper's lead football reporter, rang me one Thursday afternoon to offer me my juicy assignment, telling me to get myself to the Chinese consulate immediately to apply for my visa: we were leaving on Monday morning. It was one of Barça's first Asian tours, in the quest for what they then called emerging markets, and it took us to Seoul, Tokyo and Shanghai. We were a group of a dozen or so reporters travelling in a chartered flight alongside the team, the technical staff, a few directors and around fifty fans who had paid a princely sum to accompany the tour.

Years afterwards, I still feel privileged that I was able to be near the players, experience a world that was unknown to me and become acquainted with a group of fellow reporters who did their utmost to record the slightest incident that happened in the vicinity of the team (I also still have a Rolex watch I bought in a counterfeit market, but that is another story). *El País* asked me to report on the three games Barça were set to play and use the rest of my time to explore the cities, searching for signs of the much-publicised globalisation of football, and to write about it: the queues of Japanese fans who wanted Ronaldinho's autograph, the posters of Beckham advertising underpants in the Seoul metro, the sellers of fake Barça shirts in the markets of Shanghai...

While I followed the day-to-day life of the team during those weeks, I experienced – though quite unawares – the first moments when Messi and Ronaldinho began to connect. As some players in the squad were going to the Olympics, Frank Rijkaard had decided at the last minute to make up his squad with two B team players: Pepe Mora and Leo Messi, who had just celebrated his seventeenth birthday. I'm not a professional journalist, or a prophet, and it would be an abject lie if I said I intuited that Messi would become a great player, but it is true some of my colleagues reckoned he was more than promising, that he was working wonders in the B team, and gradually I took more notice of him in training sessions.

Messi then was the image of what would eventually become a cliché: a reserved, introverted youngster who never said a word. He was so shy he seemed scared. You never saw him alone, but neither was he at the centre of any rowdy partying. He laughed when everyone else laughed, and if my memory doesn't deceive me, he even tried to play down his talents, his excess of skill, so as not to upset his team-mates and stand out at his tender age. As he was a new boy, he had to carry balls and equipment to training sessions, and that task, and the fact that he looked like a lad who was still growing, gave him the air of an exploited orphan. He shared a room with Xavi during that tour and whoever made that decision knew what he was doing; I can't think of a better host to bond him to the group, to talk to him, to introduce him to the values of FC Barcelona and the privilege of playing for the first team.

I look back at the articles I wrote during that tour and see that I rarely mention Messi, but also that the only time he played for the team – a quarter of an hour, in the second game – he hit the post and scored a goal against Kashima Antlers in the national stadium in Tokyo (final result: 5-0). The star of the tour was Ronaldinho, which is what I wrote in my match report for *El País*:

> Ronaldinho, of course, is quite something else: the Brazilian already had a colony of followers in the country, but the game, which he dominated with a few brilliant moves, small touches, and a latent, generous presence throughout the 90 minutes, consolidated his legend even more. In the last phase of the game, for example, he was involved in so much that the fans on the terraces kept anticipating one of his signature goals, but when he had the best chance, after receiving a pass from Luis García and running into the penalty area, he decided to pass the ball to young Messi as if to say: "Go on, you do it."

All right, I agree, my report may be slightly OTT given that it was a friendly, but I was writing from

Tokyo, for heaven's sake. The key thing is Ronaldinho's gesture, which Messi has later repeated in other stadiums with other players. All great players know how to be generous, and perhaps it's one of the first things "young Messi" learned from the Brazilian ace. All great players, when they are starting out, look for a rabbi in the dressing room: the voice of experience who reveals the ins-and-outs of the squad, the team rituals, someone who passes on the philosophy behind their game and the right attitude on the pitch. It's very likely that Xavi was a good counsellor for Messi, on that trip, but however unlikely it may seem, Ronaldinho immediately assumed the mantle of his footballing rabbi.

Two years earlier, when he was playing in the junior teams, Saviola had also taken an interest in that kid everyone spoke of so highly. He had even given him his shirt. They were Argentines, they had that in common, but Saviola didn't have what it takes on or off the field to act as his sage. Ronaldinho – and Deco to a degree as well – grasped the youngster's potential immediately. Messi himself has talked about that: in the 2004-05 season, just after the Asian tour, he was still in the B team, but trained with the first team and now and then the manager gave him a few minutes on the field with them. He would go with his B team-mates to another area of the dressing room, until one day Ronaldinho insisted he took the empty locker next to his, and thus he became part of the inner circle. Rijkaard had no problem with that.

By 9 March 2008, the date of Ronaldinho's last competitive game with Barça, he and Messi had played together for almost three and a half years. Messi's first goal with the first team came from a Ronaldinho assist, a memorable goal that deserves a chapter of its own, being a very special moment. "I was looking for him the whole game," Ronaldinho recalled years later. "I really wanted him to score." After that first goal that connection was often repeated, in both directions, although it was almost always a Ronaldinho assist and a Messi goal. Watching those games again helps you to understand that apprenticeship better: the way in which Ronaldinho, without speaking a word, communicates joy in the game, the *humble* conviction of being the best and the satisfaction in making a pass that leads to a goal. Whenever he scored, Messi looked to celebrate with Ronaldinho, pointed to him in an act of acknowledgement, climbed on his back. In every game he learned to work in tandem with someone more experienced. Those were the years of broad smiles and long hair blowing in the wind, of a twenty-year-old body pushing itself to the limit with every move. But, after winning many titles and a Ballon d'Or, towards the end of his life with the *Blaugranes*, Ronaldinho began to have his ups and downs, which included absences and self-indulgences that let the team down – and when the Brazilian finally left, Messi inherited the number 10 shirt. And he is still wearing it.

15

INJURIES

You don't know what silence is if you've not been at the Camp Nou when Messi is fouled and doesn't immediately get up. Messi never play-acts. First comes an outburst of indignation, the whistles of a hundred thousand mothers and fathers who can see that their son, the apple of their eyes, has been pole-axed – they're expecting the referee to deliver justice and show a card, hopefully a red one, because bringing Messi down in full flight always looks dramatic, whether it's a premeditated crime or personal revenge in the heat of the moment. Then, if our boy doesn't get up at once, if he's writhing in pain on the ground, a dense silence descends over the stadium, converting it into a bell-jar. Ten seconds more and it's a state funeral. Before a minute is up, the whole ground begins to stir, a buzz grows as eyes focus on the other players' reactions, on the referee calling the medical staff onto the pitch. Television viewers have, at the very least, a close-up of the injured player, and you can see if Messi is complaining at all, if there is blood. But not inside the ground; inside the ground everyone is whispering, and not wanting to summon ill omens. There must be people who pray, who curse and insult the hitman, who count up the points we'll lose if he doesn't play for one, two or three months. If someone is listening to the radio, he becomes the official messenger on the terraces: they say it doesn't look serious, they say it's not looking too good…

The news spreads like wildfire. Each fan carries a doctor in his head. A fortnight's rest… No doubt it's muscular… That means it's a hamstring… Put him in the hyperbaric chamber… Prognoses are made according to the needs of the team at that precise moment. "Over time he's learned how to fall, it won't be anything serious," says the optimist. "That's it, he'll be out for the whole season," drones the pessimist. By character and tradition, Barça fans are accustomed to living on the brink of a psychodrama: until Cruyff, as coach, taught us to have faith, we suffered over the slightest thing. It was an attitude inherited by generations of fans who, by December, would already be saying, "this year, no chance, yet again" – or, with a bit of luck, it might not be until February. Even though all that is now buried under layers of confidence, we still fuss over Messi with the zeal of a gardener at the Royal Palace. If we see him vomit, or shout out in pain after a long run, we all watch him intently. If he touches his leg during the game, if he walks for too long staring at the ground, if he seems irritable... We suffer for him, and, if we could, we'd take on his pain and distribute it among all the fans, so he could continue playing. We suffer for him because we've seen him get injured before and it's never been easy.

Even so, almost nobody saw Messi's first injury, his first fracture. As Albert Martín Vidal explained in a report for the magazine *Líbero*, when Messi was thirteen, his peroneal tendon was snapped in a game against the Tortosan team Ebre Escola Esportiva. It was his second game for the B junior team, after waiting several weeks for his international transfer to arrive from Argentina. In the very first minute – there is a video – young Messi received the ball on the wing, tried to dribble and lost possession. From the

133

throw-in, a player on the other team went to punt the ball away from his defensive area and, when he was about to do so, Messi unexpectedly stuck his leg in the way and felt the full impact of the opponent's boot. That player, Marc Baiges, didn't realise until years later, when Vidal's report came out, that he had once broken Leo Messi's leg. Nor did he realise, of course, that his random act had almost changed the course of history as we know it. Messi was in plaster and on crutches for three months. That season he and his family were living in a flat the club had provided in the Les Corts area of the city, but his mother and siblings had returned to Rosario because they couldn't adapt to life in Barcelona. His father wasn't greatly convinced either and one day he sat down with his son – who was bored because he wasn't playing – and asked him if he wanted to pack his bags and return home. A word from him and he'd buy the tickets. "No, Dad. I want to succeed in Barcelona," was young Messi's reply. He was clear on that front.

Who knows if it is the memory of those tough months, or simply because he cannot stand not playing – being in dry dock, as the journalistic cliché goes – but Messi suffers a great deal when he's injured. The first big injury of his professional career was muscular, and boded ill; it happened on 7 March 2006 during a Champions League game against José Mourinho's Chelsea. He broke the biceps femoris in his right leg. Two and a half months out and, worse still, it meant he couldn't play in the final in Paris. The sad sight of a woeful Messi embracing Frank Rijkaard on his way to the dressing room was to be repeated two years later, in March 2008, in another Champions League game, against Glasgow Celtic. In the meantime he'd had other muscular injuries, in the league and with the national team, but this one was particularly painful. There were uncontrollable tears, and feelings of powerlessness, because three months earlier he'd suffered a very similar injury against Valencia. These are the moments when the Camp Nou falls silent and fans start to suffer.

Besides, all those injuries began to create the feeling that something was wrong. The media started to speculate, wondering whether those weak muscles weren't a result of misguided hormone growth treatment (the doctors replied that they weren't). He should handle his body better, they argued. He should know how far he can or can't push it, they said.

The truth is that Pep Guardiola's arrival as manager in 2008 worked wonders for him for a couple of years, starting with a change of diet. Fewer pizzas and huge Argentinian *milanesas a la napolitana*, with their greasy meat deep-fried in breadcrumbs. In 2013, however, after a year in which he suffered four injuries, Messi placed himself in the hands of an Italian nutritionist, Giuliano Poser, who advised an even more radical change in his diet, with the aim of getting the best out of each muscle and at the same time preventing injury. It consisted of carefully choosing what to eat, a diet based on whole, unprocessed ingredients, like olive oil, seasonal fruit, fresh fish – and the less pre-prepared, the better. Since then, Messi has had several more injuries – the worst was in September 2015, a strained ligament, two months out – but none as serious as those he had ten years ago (touch wood!).

Apart from his physical condition, some of these injuries are the result of fouls committed by opponents who don't always gracefully accept his ability to dribble, or who badly miscue their tackles. In September 2010, for example, in a game against Atlético Madrid, the defender Ujfalusi hit Messi's right ankle so hard – a straight red card – that Messi's medial collateral ligament was damaged. He was out for two weeks and images of his ankle, swollen like a tennis ball, went around the world.

It's uncanny – or maybe not – that Real Madrid players should figure large among the circle of Messi's usual aggressors, especially in the period when they were managed by Mourinho. It's true that the rivalry is intense, and that Messi usually plays extremely well against the *Merengues* – just ask Iker Casillas, their erstwhile goalkeeper, who would bite his lip and look into the heavens whenever he was forced to collect the ball from the back of the net – but we have often witnessed aggression that seems to spring from personal frustration. Marcelo and Pepe have left their mark, and Sergio Ramos has twice been sent off for heavy-duty tackles on Messi that bore the hallmark of fury.

Nowadays, with a 31-year-old Messi, every game he doesn't play is a cause for regret in the footballing world. Moments we will never recover. His injuries are a footballing memento mori, reminding us that one day Messi will never play again, that we'll look for him on the turf – just as his companions, perhaps, instinctively seek him out, when he is injured – and he won't be there any more. Then (bring on the violins) "for a few seconds we stand above an abyss, and common sense tells us that our existence is but a brief crack of light between two eternities of darkness..."

All right, all right, no need to exaggerate, I'm only mentally preparing for the day he will never play again.

16

NON-FICTION

BEFORE MESSI WE NEVER THOUGHT ABOUT records. Statistics, the minutiae of everyday football expressed in numbers, were of very little interest, the opposite of what we liked most. We preferred to be excited by what had never been done before, or by what nobody else can do.

This mania for statistics comes from the United States, where the output of sports stars and teams is calculated to the nth degree in the whimsical hope that the future can be predicted. And there is a partial explanation: in a normal baseball league season a team plays 162 games in six months, that is, an average of six games a week. In the NBA, a basketball team has to play a minimum of 82 games per season, and 110 if it reaches the final. There are few fans with the time to keep abreast of them all. League-table positions are revised more than once a day, according to the country's different time zones, and at the end of the championship the teams who rise to the top are those who establish a more regular rhythm.

Numbers and statistics are the non-fiction of football, the cold, impersonal traces that years later try to explain history – what happened. And yet that's not the reality we remember. For example, does anyone know how that match against Getafe ended when Messi scored that goal? I'm sorry: that Goal. Every movement is etched on our brain, with that shot as the goalie comes out, Eto'o running alongside, tracking the move, putting his hands to his head in astonishment, the celebration with team-mates... Few remember that the final result was 5-2. Who scored the other goals? Ah, that's a mystery. The game was a Copa del Rey Semi-final, and people remember even less of the return leg: three weeks later, Barça lost at Getafe's ground – a massive 4-0 – and were eliminated. Rijkaard had left Messi to rest in Barcelona, and it was a disastrous night for the fans. In the bureaucratic log of figures, Messi's goal gets buried as something futile.

Lebron James, a great player in the NBA, says that

records only exist to be beaten. And I dimly remember that, when he managed the Dream Team, Johan Cruyff used to joke that statistics exist to be disproved. In fact, the importance of these figures only comes to light when someone surpasses them, which is another of Messi's footballing virtues. Beyond the documentary footprint, I like to think that some players enter posterity through the record book, and that one day they will again be the focus of attention when at last they lose their crown. Telmo Zarra, for example, Athletic Bilbao's legendary forward, held the record as highest goalscorer in the Spanish league with 251 goals for almost 60 years, until Messi passed that number in 2014. Sometime before that the Argentine surpassed the highest goalscorer for Barça, César, who had held the record since 1955 with 232 goals. And Gerd *Torpedo* Müller, the German who played for Bayern Munich in the 1970s, watched as Messi snatched two of his records. First, in 2012, he beat his goal tally for a calendar year: Müller had scored 85 in 1972, and Messi reached 91. And later on, in January 2018, he surpassed him in goals scored in one top-flight league: the *Torpedo* stopped at 365 in the Bundesliga and, with a goal from a free kick against Real Sociedad, Messi reached 366 in La Liga. At the end of the season the figure was 383. Since then the number has reached 415 (April 2019). And life goes on.

I'm noting these figures, which are only a small selection of the records that Messi holds, and I can't help yawning because I am so bored. The hunt for records may be an insatiable paraphilia for some football fans. There will always be another possibility, another obscure statistic to beat, personally and collectively...

When he was about to celebrate his 50th birthday, the writer Enrique Vila-Matas, a Barça club member from birth, wrote a piece in which he spoke about his aversion to round numbers and the "unjustified, absurd prestige" we give them: he was defining the boredom sometimes provoked by yet another random celebration. At the beginning of 2018, Messi scored the 4,000th goal in competitive games played at the Camp Nou. Well, great. Three days later Luis Suárez scored number 4,001 against Deportivo Alavés, and even though it was crucial because it started a fight back, it was denied the halo of glory.

I'm not saying that I don't have an occasional interest in records, or anniversaries, or round numbers, but I prefer them when they are accompanied by a fantastic move, when that chance occurrence is merely an added extra. A fabulous example was Messi's 500th goal in a competitive match, which he scored on 23 April 2017, in no lesser place than the Santiago Bernabeu, on one of the most memorable nights in recent years for fans of the *Blaugranes*. Barça and Madrid were drawing 2-2. I'm sure you recall the moment. It's the 92nd minute and everything seems signed and sealed when Sergi Roberto starts a run from midfield. Nobody stops him, and he opens it up on the left for André Gomes. The Portuguese player stops, makes a short pass to Jordi Alba, who is racing up the pitch, and Alba crosses the ball with his first touch. Then Messi appears from nowhere, the world suddenly seems to stop for a tenth of a second, waiting for the cosmos to sort itself out and everything to return to its rightful place, and Messi shoots inside the penalty area, through a forest of legs, slamming it into a corner of the goal, and it is 2-3. I doubt whether Messi was thinking, right then, that he was scoring goal number 500 of his career, at least not when he took the shot – but immediately after, to celebrate, he gestured in a way that did seem premeditated, and it was an iconic gesture that would be on the front page of all the morning papers, because it summed up the emotion of the game and his epic, almighty presence: Messi takes off his shirt and shows it to the terraces of the Bernabeu. Serene and proud, as if to say: "I am *the* number 10".

In the post-match press conference, his coach Luis Enrique commented: "Messi is key even when he's at home having dinner."

Among the sequence of images that have stuck from that night, just after the goal, you can see Cristiano Ronaldo shake his head angrily, and it's at this point that records and statistics begin to interest me a little. For years those who defend CR7 have resorted to figures to compare him to Messi, not realising that football is much more than that, and even extends beyond the rivalry between two brands, Nike and Adidas. As John Carlin said in *El País*, Cristiano is a natural centre forward – "the best 9 in the world" – which he has demonstrated in the recent phase of his career, but Carlin also says it would do him good to learn to laugh at himself, "because he is a 9 that will never make it to 10".

The first theatre of conflict for these two players is the Ballon d'Or. Both have won it five times; in fact, they shared it between them over the decade from 2008 to 2017. We must go back to 2007 to find a different winner: the Brazilian Kaká (and on that distant occasion Cristiano came second and Messi third). This duel was only interrupted in 2018 by the unexpected appearance of Luka Modrić, who carried off the trophy in recognition of his decisive presence in Real Madrid's Champions League victory of 2017-18, and in Croatia's progression to the World Cup Final in Russia. Even though Modrić had his obvious merits, Messi had undoubtedly enjoyed a great season: he won the Golden Shoe as the top goalscorer in Europe and also made the most assists in La Liga. It's likely that, once again, he was being penalised excessively for the dismal performance of the Argentinian national team.

Ignoring this quasi-random parenthesis with Modrić, throughout the ten years of Messi and Cristiano domination, their rivalry has increasingly became a focus for the media and both have kept on breaking records. What's more, there are still several records that can change hands while they both continue to play. Highest goalscorer in the history of the Champion's League, for example: in 2015 both surpassed Raúl González's historic record of 77 goals, and currently (May, 2019) Cristiano has scored 126 and Messi 112. Both have scored eight hat-tricks in Europe's elite competition. In La Liga Messi has scored three goals on 33 occasions and Cristiano, 34…

You see? I'm yawning again. And that's without a mention of their national teams, Argentina and Portugal. Rather than rummaging in the archives of this personal duel for more data in favour of one or the other, perhaps it's worthwhile remembering that Messi is slightly younger and will probably enjoy more time playing at an international level. Two or three years, perhaps five – an eternity to beat every record and ensure that people shut up about them for ever and ever. Amen.

17

SMILES AND TEARS*

FAME WENT BEFORE HIM FROM A very early age. Everyone had seen or wanted to see the footballer who scored four or five goals a match, often against much older opponents. Anyone who had seen him play, let alone anyone who had coached him, made much of this privilege and dared make predictions about his future. He had been outstanding at different club levels and when the Catalan TV Channel 33 showed a Barça B game on a Saturday afternoon, viewing figures rocketed. Given his credentials, it's hardly surprising that we don't remember just one Messi debut, as with other players, but several. In fact, whenever I say his first game with the Barça first team was against Porto,

*The title in Spain of the film, *The Sound of Music*.

151

in a friendly, under Frank Rijkaard, many people correct me and say that's wrong, it was in a preseason match, the Gamper Trophy, at the Camp Nou. Against Juventus. However, that was what you might call an apocryphal debut. Memory is capricious and naturally selects one of the first days when Messi stood out and impressed us all; it was a dazzling, festive occasion that felt historic. It's reasonable enough because it was the day when he made his debut in the starting line-up, and, from the first minute, with the game before him like a blank page, he was able to display a sample from his catalogue of wondrous wares. You may remember the date: 24 August 2005.

I should add that circumstances turned the game into a contest of smiles and tears, but first we should go back a week, to 17 August, when he made his debut in the Argentinian national team, and it didn't exactly go well.

Argentina were playing a friendly against Hungary. José Pékerman, the manager, was intending to try out new players, but everyone knew he wanted to give Messi his debut. He was just eighteen and would be the youngest player to start for the first team. The game was progressing, Argentina were winning 1-2 and Messi came onto the pitch in the 64th minute, with number 18 on his back, substituting for the forward Lisandro López. Take a look at the images, if possible while listening to some horror movie musical. Messi walks out and stands near the halfway line. He immediately receives the ball and passes it to D'Alessandro, who loses it. A few seconds later someone wins it back. The ball comes to Messi again, who takes it forward. A Hungarian midfielder, Vanczák, comes after him, grabs his shirt and fouls him. Messi tries to disentangle himself, stops, waves his arms, and the Hungarian falls to the ground as if he has been lethally elbowed in the face, and starts feeling to see if blood has been drawn. The German referee is close to the incident, and without a second thought shows Messi a red card. Nobody can believe it, it must be a joke. The Argentinian players crowd around the referee. It's as if they were saying: "You donkey, can't you see you have just unfairly sent off the guy who will be the best player in history? Do you really want that blot on your copybook?" Meanwhile, Messi does nothing; he seems gobsmacked, looks at the referee from afar, and, incredulous and frustrated, pulls his shirt out of his shorts, baring his midriff. D'Alessandro, who played for Wolfsburg at the time and spoke a bit of

153

German, confronts the referee and says: "Why do you want to hog the limelight? Don't you know it's the lad's debut game?" As nothing can be done, Messi walks slowly and despondently towards the touchline. He's been on the pitch how long? Forty-seven seconds? It's a gross injustice. At the end of the game, when the rest of the team goes back to the dressing room, Messi is a sobbing mess.

Today that seems like a ridiculous mistake, almost an anecdote to entertain friends over after-dinner drinks, but at the time it turned the player's world upside down. Even the opponent Vanczák later said the red card was too severe. As for the referee, I can't decide whether to name and shame him or keep his identity quiet. What would be for the best? To penalise him with anonymity and not even connect him to Messi? Or fully expose him, as redress for his blatant, arrogant over-reaction? The previous year, the UEFA had named him the world's best referee. His name was Markus Merk – there you have it – a dentist by profession, and his track record shows him to have been some kind of red-card psychopath.

Seven days later Messi walked out to play in the Joan Gamper Trophy against Juventus, but we shouldn't discount the idea he was also playing against fate that evening, as if a good performance could erase the bad taste left by his Argentina debut. We also know that, in those days, club members were lured to the Gamper by the prospect of seeing the next season's new players. The first game of the summer was also the time to greet fans in neighbouring seats, get acquainted with new signings and start assessing future potential.

That afternoon Messi wore number 30, as he did the whole season; it was progress of sorts as Ronaldinho was number 10 and Deco number 20. In the sixth minute he made his first move down the right, with a dummy that left his marker, Pessotto, on the floor, before putting in a dangerous cross, which Larsson couldn't convert into a goal. The Camp Nou spontaneously erupted in an "Oh!" and the Rai Uno commentator said: "*Messi ha già fatto vedere un numero di alta scuola*" (I've left it in Italian because it has a nobler ring). The Juve players, who were still ambling at a pre-season pace, realised that the youngster was running rings around them and started fouling him viciously. By the 35th minute the Italians had been shown three yellow cards and two others had been given warnings. Spurred on by their aggression, Messi took possession of the ball and took them on. He was insatiable. Figures like Cannavaro, Del Piero and Ibrahimović contemplated his frantic, rather out-of-control derring-do, while his team-mates simply helped out by passing him the ball. The crowd cheered every move, every touch, every turn. Messi barely shot, but in the 66th minute he sent a long pass Iniesta's way that led to the equaliser (Del Piero had previously scored from the penalty spot). Fabio Capello coached that Juventus side and later revealed that, in the middle of the game, after watching Messi's flurry of passes, he went over to Rijkaard and told him he wanted to sign Messi on loan there and then.

At some point in the second half, the Camp Nou began to chant: "Messi, Messi, Messi…" to reward a display that lacked only a goal, and I imagine it's not often a player provokes such enthusiasm from his first steps on the pitch. Rijkaard rewarded him by taking him off in the last minute of the game, and as he left the pitch, the fans applauded, welcoming the birth of a star.

There was an element of red tape behind Capello's loan request: Messi had yet to acquire Spanish nationality and couldn't play for the first team because the quota of foreign players had been met. The second his papers came through a month later, Rijkaard included him in the line-up in a Champions League match against Udinese, and he gradually started to appear on the team-sheet, often replacing Giuly. A few weeks later, for example, Messi was in the starting line-up at the Bernabeu, in a league game that Barça won 0-3, with a dazzling display by Ronaldinho that was applauded by Real Madrid fans entranced by his genius – while their team of waning stars like Zidane, Roberto Carlos and Ronaldo (*il Fenomeno*, not CR7) stood and watched. The times were a-changing.

FC Barcelona also updated Messi's contract twice over those months, readjusting it in light of their expectations and considering his status as a player with full rights to a first-team place. Perhaps that's why two other debuts, which at the time were especially decisive, went unnoticed. The first was his official premiere in the league, in October 2004, in Montjuïc against RCD Espanyol, but the second was more momentous: scoring his first goal for the first team. It was 1 May 2005 – Labour Day – and they were playing against Albacete at the Camp Nou. Barça were two games away from winning La Liga and took the lead 1-0. With just four minutes left to the final whistle, Messi came on for

Eto'o and it was immediately obvious he was hungry. Generous as ever, Ronaldinho started playing for him, got the ball, scooped a pass over the defence and Messi scored with a gentle chip over the goalkeeper. The referee ruled it out as offside, even though it wasn't, but that was all for the better, because one minute later Messi received a pass from Deco, played it to Ronaldinho, who returned the ball with the same scooped pass as before, and Messi scored again with a gentle chip over the goalie. This time it counted, a real blockbuster of a goal celebrated by everyone as if they'd uncorked a bottle of champagne that would never run dry. You see: Messi had to score his first goal twice. From the very beginning he challenged one of the golden rules of football: there shall be no two moves alike. Well, in his realm, there could be.

18

FICTION

MANY FANS HAVE GROWN UP WITH Leo Messi and the Harry Potter novels. In 1997, Messi was ten and Harry Potter, eleven, and both were already making magic. There are readers, then, who have matured with them, one season after another, one book after another, and become adults with them. More than one might think, in retrospect, the journey pursued by Messi's Barça could also be a fiction powered by a superhero, another lad with a divine touch. After growing up with the junior teams, being part of a kind of Hogwarts that goes by the name of La Masia, he passed various tests, always accompanied by a group of friends and a circle of coaches who prepared him for increasingly complex challenges.

Naturally, for a long time the narrative has been

heading towards a happy ending. At this point (April 2019), Messi has played 33 finals as a player and won 23 of them. If you want to describe his evolution, you must occasionally draw on your skills as a storyteller. As you move away from the strictly factual, from statistics, calendars and records, Messi calls for a new language, a different discourse, narrative innovations that match the innovations of his style of play.

When I told friends that I was writing these pages, many asked: "Have you interviewed him? Have you met him?" The first response is, of course, no. Every journalist knows it is extremely difficult to interview Leo Messi. I'd then add that I would have liked to, but without much conviction. The Messi I know, the one almost all of us know, is a real Messi who has quite unintentionally transformed himself into a powerful fiction. He is a Messi with feelings and emotions. We have suffered with him when he's been injured and mentally hugged him whenever he has scored or held up a cup. And the paradox is: the more international his fame, the more global the phenomenon, the closer you feel to him, the more human he seems. What's more, if you live in Barcelona there's always the chance you might bump into him at a Latin music concert, an

Argentinian barbecue restaurant or a theatre watching a Ricardo Darín play.

The truth is we know very little about the real-life Messi, behind closed doors at home with his family. He sometimes posts images on social media: the swimming pool where he plays with his children, the sofas where he takes a siesta surrounded by his dogs, or holidays on a yacht with his wife, Antonella, and a few friends... As writer Sergi Pàmies put it, "Messi is a big mystery" and we fill out that mysterious space with our imaginings. That's why the imaginative potential is as broad and unknown as all those hours he spends off the pitch. Sometimes, when I'm looking at the blurred videos of Messi when he was seven, dribbling around other kids on dusty wasteground in Rosario, I think he could be a hero in Peter Weir's film, *The Truman Show*: his life filmed so we can admire him, sometimes feel for him, just be with him. Then I remember the night he was presented with his second Ballon d'Or, in January 2011, in Zurich, when he was a finalist along with Iniesta and Xavi – who had won the World Cup the year before with the Spanish team. Messi wasn't expecting to win, he was convinced it wasn't his turn, and he looked gobsmacked as he went on stage to receive the award from the hands of Pep Guardiola. Overwhelmed by the moment, he gave special thanks to his team-mates. It had been an unexpected twist in the script, even though everyone else – Iniesta and Xavi included – knew it was the most logical.

On the pitch, however, Messi the creator is always in control of what is happening around him and the scope for self-expression is wide open. He sometimes plays with his imagination and plucks out of the hat unexpected, almost science-fiction solutions. Other times he goes all postmodern and attempts variations on a well-known theme, such as when he comes in from the wing, parallel to the penalty area, dribbling around several players until he finds a gap: then his shot takes his opponent (and us) by surprise, because it can go right or left, be a piledriver or a billiard-cue touch, seeking out the angle of the crossbar or lobbing over the goalie – but it is always a goal. Sometimes he pulls the strings, initiating the move, combining with his midfield team-mates, and suddenly it's choreographed and the football takes on a sensuous harmony – summed up by football commentator Joan Maria Pou on RAC1 radio station as one of those moments when the game becomes "an erotic fiesta, with everyone feeling themselves up a bit".

Messi is fated to be an atemporal figure in the game of mirrors that is modern football. He is a figure both intimate and remote, bound by the straitjacket of tactics yet exhibiting the freedom of an anarchic spirit. An alternative world lives in our imagination and he nourishes it. Who knows whether one day it will be possible, through videogames and virtual reality, to create a fable about a league where players travel through time and the tactics in vogue, so that we'll be able to see amazing line-ups, experiments like those attempted – in real life – by the Cosmos, that 1970s New York team, when it signed stars like Pelé, Beckenbauer, Carlos Alberto, Neeskens... My mouth waters at the thought and I think how I would have liked to see an Argentinian team managed by Marcelo Bielsa in his pomp, surrounding Messi with the ideal players to construct a game at once fabulous and rational, Ardiles and Kempes, Redondo and Bochini... Or a team in which Messi plays next to van Basten, or could combine in midfield with Sócrates and Cruyff, or open the game up wide with Garrincha and Kubala... I mentally rehearse these alternatives – past and present mingling with the future – and I'm dying to see them, but then reality bites and I see sense: what about Xavi, Iniesta,

Piqué, Busquets, Alves, Mascherano, Abidal, Valdés, Puyol, Ronaldinho, Villa, Deco and so many others? I mean, I wonder, haven't Messi and friends already given us that and much more? All power to the imagination.

19

TATTOOS

IT'S WELL KNOWN THAT MOST FOOTBALLERS don't have the gift of the gab, but their skin speaks like an open book. Whether they have anything interesting to say is another matter. When did we start taking it for granted that tattoos were the natural complement to a footballer's image? All signs indicate that the fashion came from the United Kingdom, but, as far as I know, while they were playing, neither George Best nor Paul Gascoigne – to mention two rebels – had tattoos, or at least not in an area visible to everyone. Nor did Maradona. Nor did Cruyff. And while we're at it, nor did Jonah Lomu, the legendary New Zealand rugby star, have any Maori tattoos when he played for the All Blacks, and he was a real Maori. The majority of these players got their tattoos later, in the '90s, when other younger players made it an accessory that apparently gave them more individuality. It happened more or less at the same time as when porn stars started to decorate their bodies, but that's probably another story.

If we're talking about rebellious players, with lots of attitude on and off the field, we should remember Eric Cantona in the early '90s, when he played for Manchester United (with his shirt collar turned up). He did have a tattoo then, but didn't display it: it was on his chest, at the level of his heart: the head of a Native American wearing a feather headdress. A tribal image representing leadership, struggle and commitment to his people. It may be that at some point that Native American, which now looks like a simple sketch, inspired David Beckham, with whom Cantona shared a dressing room. Beckham was the player who really initiated tattoos for publicity purposes and as a point of connection with fans. I'm here, look at me.

There are footballers who create trends and, suddenly, all their professional colleagues dress the same way, comb their hair the same way and watch the same television series. That's what happened with Beckham and, following him, almost instantaneously, hundreds of players across the world decided to turn their body

into a tableau: they filled every centimetre of their
skin with friezes, shields, religious crosses, messages
in Latin, dates in Roman numerals, quotes from the
Bible, Chinese pictograms, Walt Disney cartoons...
Anything went, and naturally those who first joined
the rush made more than one absurd spelling mistake.
Not to mention those over-enthusiastic players, who,
in order to please the fans, tattooed the badge of their
team on their hide, convinced that meant they would
never leave (and, yes, they were transferred at the end
of the season).

As for Leo Messi, his interest in tattoos has grown
over the years – in quantity and quality of design, as
his image has become more global. The British tabloids
are the best place to follow this evolution. They devote
many pages to enlightening their readers as to the icons
adorning their idols. However, Messi usually trusts
his personal tattooist, Roberto López, to interpret the
latent symbolism. Thus, the first tattoo was of a family
nature: a portrait of his mother, Celia, observes us dis-
creetly from his left shoulder-blade. She has the saintly
face of a suffering mother.

Messi wears a symbolic composition on his right
arm that could be called *Both Worlds*. On the one hand,

the outer side is adorned with ornate flourishes from Gaudí's Sagrada Família, inspired by the main rose-window of the façade of the Birth, evoking the city that has welcomed him. This is accompanied by an orange lotus flower – that can grow anywhere according to Japanese tradition – and a watch to indicate the passage of time. In the background, there's a map that puts Europe and South America into relief: his biographical connection. On the inside of his arm, a rosary recalls the city where he was born, Rosario de Santa Fe, and a flower bud represents his older son, Thiago. Further up, on the muscle at his shoulder, an image of Jesus Christ on the Cross seeks refuge under the sleeve of his shirt: it is extremely realistic, with a crown of thorns, drops of blood streaming down his temples and two piercing blue eyes. In fact, it is so vivid, it seems the footballer is atoning for artistic outrages that are not his: the thousands of tattoos pullulating across the world, often inexpertly drawn on the skin of his followers. An army of Messis in Barça's blue and garnet red colours, or Argentina's white and sky blue, tattooed on backs, arms and legs, celebrating a goal, lifting a cup, dribbling with their own shadows...

Looking at the left side of his body, we could say

that, over time, his leg has been transformed into a palimpsest. Years ago he had tattooed on his calf a life-size reproduction of the hands of his son Thiago when he was newly born, and later he encircled everything with a winged heart. On the shin, the scene was completed by a sword flanked by a football and the number 10. In the summer of 2016, coinciding with the emotional turmoil after losing the Copa América, Messi dyed his hair blond and, perhaps to give balance, dyed his whole leg black below the knee, like a sock pulled up, leaving only the football and his shirt number visible from the front, and in contrast making his son's hands stand out at the back. It wasn't mourning black; he just wanted to be more fierce and threatening. "He's become a Maori warrior," his tattooist declared.

The latest addition is a much more restrained tattoo: the red lips of his wife, Antonella Roccuzzo, that represent a kiss from her more or less at waist level. They both posted a photo on social media and, if you wanted to interpret it, you'd say it is in line with Messi's evolution as a public figure – it is more open and more visible, but with a hint of the risqué, and that is something new.

Of course, we shouldn't discount the possibility that

there may be an image consultant behind all this. There are fewer and fewer players who don't have tattoos, people like Iniesta, Sergi Roberto, Xavi, Ter Stegen, and, unexpectedly, Cristiano Ronaldo – although in his case the decision may be conditioned by the way he chooses to showcase himself: a tattoo on the muscular, body-builder's physique he bares whenever he scores a big goal would be like grime or graffiti on Michelangelo's *David*.

20

I REMEMBER

I REMEMBER THAT THE SCHOOL WHERE Messi started playing, was – and still is – called Malvinas Argentinas.

I remember that Zlatan Ibrahimović said in an interview: "If they give me the Ballon d'Or one day, the next morning I'll send it to Leo Messi."

I remember that when Barça beat Arsenal in the Champions League Final in Paris in 2006, Messi didn't collect his medal or the cup with the rest of the team; he was really sad because he'd been injured for two months and hadn't recovered in time to play.

I remember that when Messi and his father came to Barcelona in 2000, they stayed in room 546 in the

Catalonia Plaza Hotel in Plaça d'Espanya, and from time to time an idolising customer will ask to sleep in that same bedroom.

I remember Pernía, the defender who played for Atlético Madrid, also an Argentine: in one game Messi destroyed him with a dummy in midfield, one of those where he swerves his body, does nothing, and the defender is so thrown off balance he gives him free passage. Messi then began a straight run, dodged three more opponents and finished it all with a shot that hit the bar. Years later Pernía explained on television that, when he got home, his wife asked him: "What did Messi do to you?" and he replied: "I don't know, you tell me, you watched it."

I remember that, when he won his third Ballon d'Or, Messi shared the trophy with his friend Xavi, who was a finalist. "You deserve this too and it's a pleasure for me to be alongside you on the pitch," he told him.

I remember the spectacular yet subtle nutmeg Messi played on James Milner, in a Champions League game against Manchester City, and I remember Pep

Guardiola, in the stands at the Camp Nou, rubbing his face as if he was seeing visions.

I remember hearing this story long ago: when Messi was six and played in the neighbourhood team, the coach used to give the players one of those filled pastries they call *alfajores* for every goal they scored, and two if it was a header. More than once Messi dribbled past the goalkeeper, reached the goal line and, if he had time, stopped, kicked the ball up and headed it in so he'd get two *alfajores*.

I remember that two months after his fabulous goal against Getafe, where he nigh on reproduced Maradona's goal against England in the Mexico '86 World Cup, Messi emulated the Argentine idol once again. On this occasion, he scored a goal with his hand against Espanyol and everyone recalled that famous "hand of God".

I remember that, when commenting on Messi's famous goal against Getafe, Xavi laughed and said that he ought to claim the merit of the assist, even though he was 55 metres from the goalmouth.

I remember that, apart from the red card he was shown on his debut for the Argentinian national side, Messi has never been sent off in his entire career.

I remember that when Messi was given a 21-month jail sentence for tax evasion, we all breathed an immediate sigh of relief when it was reduced to a hefty fine, which meant he would avoid having to spend any time inside.

I remember Iniesta's vital goal at Stamford Bridge in the Champions League Semi-final against Chelsea, and how it was a Messi assist. He'd previously received the ball and had looked to shoot – with his right foot – but faced with three defenders, he couldn't see a way through, so had the brilliant idea of passing to Iniesta.

I remember that, after a wonderful Messi night, the Argentinian sporting daily *Olé* changed the design of its masthead, and for one day it said *Leo*.

I remember the *other* Lionel Messi, a youngster from Cameroon who plays as centre half for AS Portet, in the French second regional division. When he signed a contract, the local press couldn't resist the headline: "Messi signs for Portet!"

I remember that young boy from Afghanistan who had made an Argentinian national team shirt from a plastic bag and painted a 10 and Messi's name on the back with a ballpoint pen. Shortly after he was invited to the Camp Nou for a friendly game against Al-Ahli and Messi presented him with a real shirt.

I remember that great basketball player, Stephen Curry, before an important contest between his team the Warriors and the Blazers, conjuring up Leo Messi's mentality in order to win the game.

I remember that Messi really likes his sleep.

I remember that Messi still hasn't scored directly from a corner, what's called an Olympic goal. He's tried several times, but the post or the goalie always got in the way. In training, however, he's managed it more than once.

I remember that Nike advert with other players he did when he was seventeen and that at the end he took a free kick and said: "Remember my name, Leo Messi." And I remember that Jonathan dos Santos also appeared in that advert.

I remember how, during the celebrations for the treble in 2009, which included a cavalcade through the streets of Barcelona, the players drank lots of beer. At the Camp Nou, a tipsy, reckless Messi, wearing a beret, grabbed the microphone and promised that next year they would win everything, every single title. Guardiola buried his head in his hands.

I remember that when Messi didn't renew his contract with Barça, and everything was up in the air, I thought of Manchester City with Pep Guardiola, Txiki Begiristain and Ferran Soriano all there, and was convinced that one day he would join them.

I remember reading that sometimes, when they are at home with the family, his son Thiago calls him "Messi" and not "Dad".

I remember the Argentinian actor Ricardo Darín recounting how one day Messi was his cab driver. He was crossing the Carrer d'Aragó in Barcelona, and a car hooted, Darín went over and saw it was Messi, and the footballer offered to drive him to the hotel where he was staying.

I remember that when Kobe Bryant played for the US basketball team, he wore the number 10 "in honour of the most extraordinary athlete I have ever seen, Leo Messi".

I remember the death of Tito Vilanova, in April 2014, how sad the players were and how they cried at the funeral. A few days after, it transpired that Messi went to visit him just before he died, and Tito persuaded him to stay at Barça for the rest of his career.

21

THE WORLD CUP
OR WHAT NEXT AFTER RUSSIA?

For the last four years, after losing in that World Cup Final against Germany in the Maracaná stadium in the summer of 2014, many of us Messi followers tried to delude ourselves with a question full of wishful thinking: will Russia be the place he finds the greatest glory? On 15 July 2018, will we see the titch play in the World Cup Final? Our Messianism had made us incorrigible. Deep down we knew that Messi's journey with the Argentinian national team had too often been a source of anxiety and frustration. For some time now, and by a considerable margin, he has been the team's top goalscorer, but even so, overall, the memories of all the games played with the white and sky blues are bittersweet. Ever since 1986, when Argentina won the

World Cup in Mexico, every Argentinian player has wanted to be Maradona, but what happens when in a way everyone believes you have done that by the age of nineteen?

The fact is that, over time, the excessive hopes Argentina has placed in the young promise from Barcelona have turned into even more exaggerated disappointments, and, to make matters worse, have been reinforced by the voices that mould sporting opinion in the country – starting with Diego Armando Maradona himself when he was a television commentator. Here, for example, is an extract from an article by writer Martín Caparrós, published in 2011 in the Colombian magazine *SoHo*, in the midst of one of those cyclical periods of disillusion, the sort of thing that often reads like an exercise in national psychoanalysis. In this *Diatribe against Messi*, midway between irony and self-deprecation, Caparrós reproaches him for being too nice, and says that to be a proper Argentine he should be more tyrannical, and more of a hellraiser. Just before the Copa América, the gutter press had published some stories about Messi letting his hair down in a luxury flat in Buenos Aires, a wild touch to add to his well-ordered, restrained image, and Caparrós wanted to find a glimmer of optimism there. At the same time, however, he wrote:

> [Messi] left the fatherland to stop being a dwarf, the only way he could grow was by escaping, and yet his heart is so generous – and so boring – he still tried to be Argentinian.
>
> He tries and three billion say he is; only we, his would-be compatriots, have our doubts. He hasn't fired our affection or a sense of intimacy: Messi is a guy who manages incredible pirouettes with the ball a long way from home, and then, luckily, in the World Cup, he comes back to us. And, obviously, that makes us proud – we Argentines easily feel pride, almost as easily as we like to whine and complain – but it's quite false: as if we were afraid that any moment we might be found out.

It must be very difficult to ignore all this media racket that, more often than not, comes with a good dose of sentimentality. It's not sufficient that Messi has preserved his Rosario accent, or lives in Barcelona in a kind of Rosario bubble. There will always be someone to criticise him for not singing the national anthem before playing for the national team, for not being passionate about the colours, or not committed enough.

In Europe, and especially in Barcelona, it is hard to understand such a venomous attitude, and it often seems they really don't know what he's like. That they haven't watched him as much as we have. As if it were impossible for them to follow his day-to-day feats from afar and judge his extraordinary character, his sustained excellence at levels no other footballer has ever achieved. It seems that Argentines don't have the blind faith Barcelona fans have acquired after so many years watching him play: the feeling that, while Messi is on the pitch, we will usually win. Forgive my arrogance, but it's very likely that I have seen him in more games – I miss one or two games a season at the worst – than most Argentinian football fans, even though, in the era of globalisation, distances and time zones are no longer an excuse.

This lack of faith against all the evidence contains a touch of contempt for players who go abroad, and has often been accompanied by a lack of planning on the part of the Argentinian Football Association. There's no way they can seem to recruit a manager to make the most of Messi's brilliance. What should they do? Build a team around him? Give him all the power? Treat him like just another player? Some try to put him alongside a would-be Xavi, Iniesta or Busquets, but they don't grasp that it's all about a footballing philosophy. The last coach to have a go, Jorge Sampaoli, summed it up thus, in a phrase that proved to be spot on: "We must be at Messi's level." (And in Russia, they weren't, but we'll come to that in a moment.)

Every coach tries to create the ideal conditions, but maybe these have to come from outside, and are to do with the context, and they've yet to appear, maybe now never will.

I don't think it was by chance, for instance, that in the summer of 2016, after losing the Copa América Final against Chile (and missing a penalty in the shoot-out), Messi decided on a change of image. The same night as the final, in the heat of the moment, he was answering a television journalist's questions and suddenly announced he was leaving the national team: "It seems it's not for me. Regrettably I went for it, it was what I most wanted, but it hasn't worked out. And that's that," he said sadly, his mind made up. Nonetheless, a month and a half later he put out a press statement to say that he was having second thoughts. "I love my country and this shirt too much," he declared, and Argentina breathed a sigh of relief. At the same time, Messi dyed his hair platinum blond and a few weeks later got a new tattoo on his left leg, the deadlier of the two.

Afterwards reality didn't live up to the good vibes, at least in the games with the national team, and the qualifying phase for the World Cup in Russia was a *via crucis* – with three different coaches – that wasn't resolved satisfactorily until the final game. In fact, the outcome of those last games is a good example of the schizophrenia Messi can provoke in his country's journalists and mass media. In September, after a last-minute draw that kept their hopes alive, *Olé* declared: "Messi suffers and so do we," and then went on: "There's no way to look at it positively. Argentina struggled to draw against Venezuela. The moves didn't flow and there was no reaction. Messi wasn't Messi." The team was on the edge of the abyss and had it all to play for in a game in Quito, at almost 3,000 metres above sea level, against Ecuador. The day came and they won 1-3, with Messi scoring a spectacular hat-trick, and the following day's *Olé* splashed this headline over its whole front page: "Messi is Argentinian." And on an inside page: "On a par with God."

That night, when they knew they were through, Jorge Sampaoli said: "Football owes Messi a World Cup." A few weeks later the player himself reaffirmed this in an interview in the daily newspaper *Clarín*: "I hope that football pays me what it owes me."

The truth is that his words sounded like an ultimatum. Or perhaps it was the cry of someone who knew he was probably not going to have another opportunity. Usually a footballer's professional life gives him four opportunities to play in the World Cup. A sixteen-year stretch. Only four footballers have managed to play in five: the German Lothar Matthäus, the Mexican Antonio Carbajal, the Italian Gianluigi Buffon (though in his first World Cup he didn't play a single game), and, after Russia, the Mexican Rafael Márquez. As for Argentina, the only footballer who had played in four World Cups at that point was Diego Armando Maradona, and his last – 1994 in the United States – was short and sharp, with a second positive drug test that practically signalled his farewell to football. The pool for Argentinian players is so vast it seems that the team has to be rebuilt from top to bottom every four years, and very few survive from one World Cup to the next. Perhaps this lack of continuity is also down to press and social media pressure, and for that reason there is even more merit in two Argentines making the World Cup in Russia their fourth: Javier Mascherano and Leo Messi.

If we look closely, before this last World Cup Messi had followed an upwards evolution that made him a favourite (more so than his team). In 2006, his first World Cup, the number 10 to was worn by Riquelme; Messi only played for short spells and scored a goal. Germany knocked them out in the quarter-finals. In 2010, in South Africa, when the coach was Maradona, Messi wore the no.10 and played in every game, but he never felt at ease and made next to no impact – incredibly he didn't score a goal. Once again, Germany knocked them out in the quarter-finals. In Brazil, in 2014, Messi and his team were among the favourites and came closer than ever to victory: they progressed confidently, he scored four goals, but they lost the final. Against whom? Yes, against Germany. Clearly, the *bête noire* of the Argentines in Russia would be the German steamroller. And, if at all possible, they were to be avoided in the quarter-finals. That's why the Argentines breathed a sigh of relief when Germany were eliminated. The path looked smoother. The problem, however, was that their own game wasn't coming together around Messi. A draw against Iceland, a big defeat at the hands of Croatia and, then, a last-minute victory against Nigeria put them through to the knock-out stage – what's more, with a spectacular Messi goal that combined all his qualities in terms of control, orientation and quickness. That, on its own, restored them to the attentions of the seers, of people, like me, who thought that Argentina could win the World Cup simply "because Messi deserved it".

A few days before, in an article on the *New York Review of Books* website, the Argentinian writer Gabriel Pasquini described the state of maximum excitement his compatriots experience in a World Cup period and found an explanation for it in the history books. In a nutshell: in the golden age between 1880 and 1930, Buenos Aires was the Paris of the South and Argentina the world's tenth most powerful economy. Then in the 1930s, the country was hit by a devastating crisis, from which it has never recovered, to the extent that Argentina is still waiting for someone, a hero, to restore them to that glittering era. Hence, according to Pasquini, when it comes to the state of the nation they always oscillate "between their fatalism and their magical thinking". There was a time when this heroic role was played by Maradona, and now, this someone had to be Leo Messi.

In fact, we could even say that, because of his style of play, Messi is often magical thinking incarnate, an expectation built on emotion and irrational passion. But for the very same reason he can also embody the fatalism of a whole country better than anyone else. The fatalism of missing a penalty in the first game against Iceland, for example, that meant they didn't win and were set in a less positive frame of mind.

Nor do I think that Diego Maradona's presence in the stadium helps one bit – there he was again, bloated, bawling and spaced out like Elvis in full eclipse. When Germany were losing against Mexico, the television cameras didn't focus on a swaggering Matthäus smoking a Havana cigar, and when Brazil were knocked out by Belgium, we weren't shown Pelé in a luxury box, waving his hands and shouting: "What a load of bollocks!" And yet old Diego was back on our screens reminding the Argentines that he did give them glory once, and that it comes with a price.

It goes without saying that a large swathe of the

press returned to cyclomatic mode, analysing and dissecting the mistakes made by Sampaoli and his players, sometimes even issuing threats of physical violence. Beyond Messi's personal vicissitudes, Argentina can always say they were eliminated from the last sixteen by the champions France, and that their other defeat came at the hands of Croatia, France's opponents in the Moscow final. As if playing against Messi and his lads had injected those teams with a kind of superpotency that helped them progress in a World Cup, that, in any case, hardly shone for the quality of the football.

At this point, we should return to our initial question: what next after Russia? Well, after they were knocked out by France, Mascherano announced he was retiring from the national team. Messi, on the contrary, said little about his future and went on holiday, as if keeping an ace up his sleeve. Right now, it's very unlikely that he is ruminating about Qatar in 2022, a World Cup as remote as a desert wilderness, but his mind may be turning over the Copa América that will be played in Brazil in 2019. After all, that is also one of the few titles that Messi has yet to win.

22

IMMORTAL

WHEN SPEAKING OF NABOKOV'S LITERARY DECAY, Martin Amis said that "writers die twice: once when the body dies, and once when the language dies". The simile could be adapted almost literally to footballers. "Footballers die twice: once when their body dies, and once when their game dies." The day comes when the head can still play, but the legs and body don't respond so effectively.

As, then, their game – their language – dies, good footballers are the ones who adapt to their new circumstances, shaping their style, making the most of talents that aren't deteriorating, perhaps looking for a league where they don't play so fast (but pay well) or, if not, bowing out before they become a caricature of themselves. There's nothing more dramatic than a long farewell that forces you to say: "The flesh is sad, alas, and I've scored all the goals."

Eric Cantona retired at 30, too early, and then went into cinema. In his declarations to *L'Équipe*, he explained: "I am naturally curious. Every day I need to find something new, even in the simplest things. It is a permanent state of curiosity that allows me to progress in life." Many footballers can only direct this curiosity towards football. As they have spent their whole life in the same micro-climate, when they retire they look for ways not to abandon the Indian reservation altogether. Of course, the most obvious step is to get a coaching certificate and continue walking onto pitches and into dressing rooms, and the most in-your-face is to become a television pundit (though there aren't that many who are articulate enough). There are always other alternatives. Roberto Baggio got his coaching certificate, converted to Buddhism and now devotes part of his time to humanitarian activities. Not long ago, a quite peripheral Manchester United player, Philip Mulryne, appeared in the press because he had just been ordained as a priest. Romário is a federal senator in the state of Rio de Janeiro, and George Weah, chosen as best African player of the year on three occasions, won the elections to become president of his country, Liberia, in January 2018.

What will Messi do when he no longer plays football? Perhaps I'm getting ahead of myself and first we should consider where he will finish his career. For the moment, according to the last contract renewal he signed – after months of painful waiting that seemed like years – he will play for Barça until 30 June 2021, when he will have just celebrated his 34th birthday, and he will earn 39.4 million euros per season. I do a quick calculation with my calendar and start to fret about the future: do we really only have three years to enjoy watching him play? But then I realise it's too early and that it's not time to be feeling such regrets; basically it's much more agreeable to imagine what to expect in the meantime, what kind of Messi remains to be seen and how his game – and Barça's – will change as his physical condition changes. A friend of mine, for example, is convinced that one day he will end up playing like Xavi, occupying a midfield spot where he won't need to run so much, yet can combine his unique vision of space with the precision of his passes.

Conversely, when I focus on that final date, 30 June 2021, I can't help thinking that Messi will be a year away from being able to play in another World Cup, Qatar 2022, and that perhaps his need to say goodbye to football will be postponed until after that, with or without the trophy, and that he will require a club in order to be properly fit. There is yet another question mark hovering over his future: will he go back to Argentina, and play for Newell's, his childhood club? That would no doubt be an emotional return, and years ago he did express a wish to do so, but right now it doesn't seem very likely. It could only be for sentimental reasons and, after the outcome of the World Cup in Russia, the reserves of feeling for Argentina are probably at an all-time low. Messi has too often been the sacrificial lamb atoning for the sins of the team, as Ángel Cappa put it, and that takes its toll. Besides, there are fewer and fewer players who start and end their professional careers in the same team, and that would make Messi special too.

So I'll return to my original question: what will Messi do when he no longer plays football? A large part of his talent can't be taught or passed on, and to be honest I really don't imagine him becoming a coach. After being Gardel, as Argentines like to say, he would have more to lose than to gain. Nor do I see him wanting to become an oracle like Cruyff, one of those people who are always being asked questions and enlightening us as to who and what is the best.

A unique basketball star like Michael Jordan, who retired twice, said that the desire to play never disappears. Perhaps that's why there are now games for old stagers, which have become a commercial sub-genre. My Friends against Your Friends, a way to return to your childhood footballing days – who will carry the ball, who will have first pick – and meet up with old colleagues and opponents and remember skirmishes of yore. Ronaldinho, for example, played out the last years of his career – with Querétaro and then with Fluminense – as if he was always playing in games with old stagers, displaying filigree touches, and almost always passing while looking in the opposite direction.

An important point is that the only contract that Messi has signed for life is with Adidas, which pays him an amount that has never been made public to wear the brand. So we imagine that when he retires he will still be that presence, the idea we have all forged of Messi during these glory years, and perhaps we will see him in advertising campaigns from time to time, in charity activities organised by his foundation, offering his image as the eternal youngster to just causes.

As for his absence from football fields, especially from the Camp Nou, perhaps a line from a poem that W.H. Auden wrote after the death of W.B. Yeats can help us understand it: "He became his admirers." I have no doubt at all that, when he is no longer playing, on historic days, the Camp Nou will remember him with shouts of "Messi, Messi, Messi!", almost as a way of praising the talents of other players, or a celebration of past successes. Moreover, if he is there in the terraces, we will have even more reason to celebrate him.

We can also be sure that Messi will continue to play *in absentia*, from our memories. How long will we continue seeing him, when he's no longer on the pitch? In the course of all these years and titles, this golden-age Barça have achieved a level of clockwork motion, of stylistic repetition, that has equipped us to *see* those moves in our minds. If I'm listening to a game on the radio, and commentator Joaquim M. Puyal says that Messi sends a long pass over the defenders towards Jordi Alba, I have lots of images of similar passes in my head that help me to visualise this latest example. And equally so with other passes. Piqué brings the ball out of the centre of the defence and goes on the attack. Iniesta combines with Messi on the edge of the penalty box. Ter Stegen makes a providential stop with his body when an opponent shoots from point blank range. Busquets wins the ball, pushes it forward and offers it to Rakitić... We have seen it all. We have behind us a generation of unique footballers, who have shaped our footballing imaginations. They have educated us, we could say, but fortunately have never set any limits: there is always a place for Messi's flights of fancy and Suárez's impossible shots on goal. The fortune – and misfortune – of such a style means that when a player leaves or retires, his presence lingers on. Even now I still look for Xavi in the midfield, turning on himself until he gets rid of his marker, or picture Iniesta receiving the ball before making an even better return pass, or I'm expecting Dani Alves to appear down the right to link up with Messi. And it took a long time for Mascherano and Piqué, and also Umtiti and Lenglet, to be able to keep the memory of Puyol's threatening presence from coming to mind.

So you can see, we can use subterfuges to distract ourselves and look for excuses, but one day or another we will start to wonder what life will be like without that titch on the pitch. Before we start feeling sorry for ourselves, we should take note of the words of journalist Simon Kuper: "We live in the age of Messi and perhaps the best way to spend it is to watch every match." Right now I cannot think of any better way to extend that bliss and thus forget the day when Messi will make his exit, depart the stage and become definitively immortal.

ACKNOWLEDGEMENTS

At the start of his book *Football* (Les Éditions de Minuit, 2015), Jean-Paul Toussaint writes: "This book will please nobody, neither intellectuals, who aren't interested in football, nor football fans, who will find it too intellectual. But I needed to write it, I didn't want to break the thin thread that still bonds me to the world." I've thought of Toussaint's words more than once while writing these pages about Messi. Messi? Leo Messi? Here's a book destined to oblivion, because everyone knows so much about him, so many small details and anecdotes, that no one will want to read it, and after all a video of his goals is much more exciting than any explanation I might add. Yet all the same I really wanted to prolong every moment of joy he has given me – who knows if that is also a way of bonding me to this world.

Conversely, I barely gave intellectuals a thought when I was writing. Perhaps because that unbridgeable abyss is diminishing all the time, thanks to journalists who write about football with a different perspective. For almost twenty years I have had the good fortune to write regularly about football in the press and especially about FC Barcelona. I owe everything I have learned – positioning and technique, the confidence to make a risky pass – to a few friends and masters. Pride of place should go to Ramon Besa at *El País*, who gave me the chance to kick off. Then David Torras, Albert Guasch and Eloy Carrasco, at *El Periódico*, who have never left me on the bench. Perikles Monioudis gave me an international cap at *The FIFA Weekly*. And also with the help of all their colleagues in their teams. I should also add the memories of so many friendly games at truly unruly hours: the nightly conversations on RAC1 radio at *Café Baviera* with Xavier Bosch, and more recently my exchanges on Catalunya Ràdio with Bernat Soler. I owe them all a debt of gratitude.

Jordi Puntí was born in Manlleu, near Barcelona, and is a fiction writer and regular contributor to the Spanish and Catalan press. He was also a contributor at *The FIFA Weekly*. He has won numerous literary awards and his works have been translated into more than 15 languages. His first novel to be translated into English, *Lost Luggage* (Short Books), was released in 2013, and his new collection of short stories, *This is Not America*, will be published in the US in 2019.